Psalm 119

Psalm 119

A Twenty-Two-Day Devotional Study
Designed to Help You Journey through
the Riches of This Beautiful Psalm

JONATHAN PETER BECKETT

RESOURCE *Publications* · Eugene, Oregon

PSALM 119
A Twenty-Two-Day Devotional Study Designed to Help You Journey
through the Riches of This Beautiful Psalm

Resource Publications
An Imprint of Wipf and Stock Publishers
199 W. 8th Ave., Suite 3
Eugene, OR 97401

www.wipfandstock.com

PAPERBACK ISBN: 978-1-6667-0676-5
HARDCOVER ISBN: 978-1-6667-0677-2
EBOOK ISBN: 978-1-6667-0678-9

01/10/22

www.austinmacauley.com

First Published (2021)
Austin Macauley Publishers Ltd
25 Canada Square
Canary Wharf
London
E14 5LQ

I wish to convey my thanks to John Engall and
Jim Winter, Ph.D. for their editorial advice.
I am also grateful to Ian Topalian, B.Sc., church elder,
for his support in creating this book.

I dedicate this book to my Nan (Maureen), who has been inspirational in her genuine Biblical faith in the Lord Jesus Christ—a role model of laudable emulation in her daily walk with the Lord. I wish to thank my family (Stan, Gill, Rachel, Nick, Isabella, Lucy and Jessica) for all their sincere love, support and care. Third, I would like to thank my friend, Stephen, for his care and genuine fellowship. Finally, to commend my good friends—Jeffrey, Tim, and Richard, who are faithful brothers in the Lord and a great encouragement in missional evangelism.

Contents

Preface

IN MARCH 2020, THE world was exposed to reports of COVID-19 (the coronavirus), affecting many aspects of everyday life. The aberrant bipartisan of world order and formation of alliances is testament to the asserted unification required in order to eradicate the virus. The media, at the time, reported a high death toll and potential for transmission of the virus. Consequently, people were required to conform to measures such as 'lockdown', sanitising hands and social distancing in an attempt to decrease the likelihood of catching the virus. During this era, people were asked to stay at home. It is possible, that this period of history may have caused individuals to have more time to reflect, read and ask searching questions. Certainly, when faced with the brevity of life, it is poignant to ask: what is it all about? Making time to read the Bible, especially Psalm 119, is a great benefit as it deals with the importance of life issues, chiefly, challenging: do you know and love God? Do you love His Word? Such questions may be the antithesis of secular humanism but are essential in God's economy—they are vital, eternal matters. The rationale of this book is to assist in re-calibrating our assessment of lives, priorities, as England comes out of further 'lockdown.'

Chapter 1 offers *an introduction to the study of the Psalms*, covering their authorship and their types and their purposes. Chapter 2 is a *devotional exposition of Psalm 119*, the study of the Psalm 119 itself: analysing literary features and the notion of holiness through exposition. It extrapolates from each section of the psalm as a tool to help you understand, more fully, Psalm 119. Chapter 3 is *a summary* of the key terms used in Psalm 119.

This book explores the Psalm 119. Its aim is to help your devotions through this psalm, to bless you as you meditate prayerfully upon the sections of this psalm. The Psalmist prays, with a teachable spirit, that God would speak to him. Verses 26, 64 and 66 state: 'Teach me.' Such an approach offers generalisability beyond the prayers of one person to illumine how we may find help from God, no matter what we are facing.

As a sizable psalm, compared approximately to the size of shorter Biblical books such as Ruth, James or Paul's writings to the Ephesians or Philippians, there is a significant amount to draw to the reader's attention. In so doing, this work synthesises as a backdrop, the significance of the book of Psalms, identifying the importance of studying the psalms in devotional times in a clear interpretative way from the genres or themes within them. Finally, and most significantly, this work explores the literary features of Psalm 119 and highlights the spiritual application to a Christian believer or student of the Bible, seeking enhanced understanding of the salient points in each of the stanzas and verses through Biblical exegesis.

CHAPTER 1

An Introduction to the
Study of the Psalms

THIS CHAPTER OFFERS AN *introduction to the study of Psalms. This includes the authorship of Psalms and the types and purposes of the Psalms.*

Ancient Hebrew literature consists of narrative, poetry, song, reflection, didactic reasoning, prophecy, liturgy and so forth. 'Psalm' comes from the Greek meaning a 'song' or 'hymn', the Hebrew term for the book refers to 'praises'. Moreover, McKenzie and Kaltner explain: 'The word "Psalm" comes from the Greek *Psalmos*, which is how the Greek translation, or *Septuagint* (LXX), renders the Hebrew term *mizmar* (song) that is the title of –57 compositions in the book.'[1] The Lord Jesus and the apostles called this the 'book of Psalms' (Luke 20:42; Acts 1:20). The primary aims of this book are to lead God's people as a hymn book in worship and record God's dealings with mankind. It is interesting to note how the Psalms begin with 'asher' (happy) and the blessedness of praising God (chapter 1:1) and conclude with the injunction, 'Praise ye the LORD', (Hallelujah!) (chapter 150:6). Within it, nuanced terms for God are used. For example, Psalm 14 verse 2 uses both 'Yahweh' (LORD)

---

1. McKenzie and Kaltner, *Old Testament*, 328.

and 'Elohim' (God). 'The segmented discourses in Psalm 119 use contrasts, colas, chiasms, line grouping, parallelisms, acrostic and so forth' (Brown, 2014). To highlight some examples: the number of colas ('cola' is the plural of 'colon' which refers to a terse utterance in Hebrew verse) for each line in Psalm 119 is '16' based upon 176 verses, 'representing a peak climax' structure.[2] A rhythmic pattern occurs in some Psalms where ideas are grouped together in patterns of ideas (rather than syllables). For example: Psalm 54:12 is one line divided into two stichs: 'And I will make thy windows of agates, and thy gates of carbuncles, and all thy borders of pleasant stones.' This may indicate the variable meter or show where emphasis is to be stressed when orally expressing the ideas. Second, chiastic pattern means 'to place crosswise' or in the shape of an 'X' to mirror two parallel clauses. For example, Psalm 8 follows a symmetrical chiasm: a benediction (A—verse 1), God's rule (B—verses 1–2), man's meanness (C—verses 3–4), man's greatness(C—verse 5), man's rule (B—verses 6–8) and then a benediction (A—verse 9). Synonymous parallelism can be seen in the line: 'Therefore the ungodly shall not stand in the judgment, nor sinners in the congregation of the righteous' (Psalm 1:5). This is where two lines of a verse are descriptive—the first line states the wicked will 'not stand' and this is missing from the second part, as this is inferred. A further textual literary device is antithetical parallelism—involving contrasting matters—'the evil' and those 'who hope in the LORD' (Psalm 37:9); in both cases their latter end is described. Equally, Psalm 30:5 notes God's anger and weeping at night but joy 'in the morning' (the second line contrasting with the first). Synthetic parallelism is where the second line of the Psalm completes the first (rather than repeating or contrasting). For instance, Psalm 2:5–6: God is said to rebuke in wrath, vex them, as a corrective measure. The second part denotes, how the Psalmist sets God as king of his heart (who reigns in Zion).

The lines are augmented, each line adding information. In verse 6, it defines the location (Zion) building on verse 5's description. The use of climactic parallelism, similar to synthetic parallelism,

---

2. Freedman and Geoghegan, *Psalm 119*, 20.

builds to a climax, like a staircase building upwards (one line builds upon another and links the stairs together). Psalm 93:3 states: 'The floods have lifted up, O Lord, the floods have lifted up their voice; the floods lift up their waves.' This shows how material is added to build to a climactic crescendo. Emblematic parallelism uses similes ('like' and 'as') to compare ideas: as The LORD has compassion upon His children like a father has for his son or daughter (see Psalm 103:12–13). Finally, acrostic Psalms (the most famous being Psalm 119, the focus of this work) are built using the same or successive letters of the Hebrew alphabet to give a full-perspective of a matter and to aid memorisation. A further example of this is Psalm 145 where each verse begins with the successive letter (omitting *nûn* in verses 13 and 14 as not included within the Masoretic text). The use of alphabetical structure is also applied in Lamentations 3, where a triple alphabetical structure is implemented, all three lines in each stanza opening with the corresponding letter.

The book of Psalms comprises a collection of 150 Hebrew songs and refrains of God's messages, reflective experiences of His dealings with men and His commands to men.[3] Books of the Psalter are classically divided into five books, each with a concluding doxology:

- Book 1 (Psalms 1–41)
- Book 2 (Psalms 42–72)
- Book 3 (Psalms 73–89)
- Book 4 (Psalm 90–106)
- Book 5 (Psalm 107–150).

Kidner explains how the Books of the Psalter are divided into 'blocks of material' thematically arranged within clusters of related points.[4] The appeal of the Psalms is they offer a heightened sense of worship (as they aid a believer in corporate or private devotions with better and higher words with which to praise God). Moreover, they offer theological certainty as they show some of God's works

3. Arnold and Beyer, *Encountering the Old Testament*, 282.
4. Kidner, *Psalms 1-72*, 18.

and how He rules and responds to the prayer and praise of His people. They also have a timeless aesthetic quality showing beauty coupled with grace. Furthermore, many of the Psalms have author titles ascribed to them: David is named in Psalms 3–32, 34–41, Book 1 (1–41), Psalms 51–65, 68–70, Book 2 (42–70), Psalm 86, Book 3 (73–89), Psalms 101, 103, Book 4 (90–106) and 108–10, 122, 124, 131, 133, 138–45, Book 5 (107–50), Solomon is considered as the author of Psalm 72, Book 2 (42–72) and Psalm 127, Book 5 (107–150). Asaph is ascribed to the authorship of Psalm 50, Book 2 (42–72) and Psalms 73–83, Book 3 (73–89). Next, the Sons of Korah are said to have written Psalms 42–49, Book 2 (42–72) and Psalms 84–85, 87, Book 3 (73–89). Heman, Psalm 88, Book 3 (73–89) and Ethan: Psalm 89, Book 3 (73–89). Finally, there are some 'orphan Psalms', which are anonymous, these are: Psalms 1, 2, 33, 66, 67, 71, 91–100, 102, 104–7, 111–21, 123, 125–26, 128–30, 132, 134–37 and 146–50. It has been traditionally surmised that due to the extremities David faced and the literary features of Psalm 119 that this Psalm is penned by David.[5] For the purpose of this work, I shall adopt this position and use David, the writer, the Psalmist and so forth interchangeably.

As well as the names of the authors, some psalms have titles of the literary or musical genre: song (shir) refers to the songs sung either unaccompanied or with musical instruments. Some of the songs were sung on pilgrimage 'up to' Jerusalem (songs of ascents or degrees-*shi hamma'aloth*). 'Psalms' (*mizmor*) is used 57 times as a verb 'to play', referring to musical accompaniment to the singing of the psalm. A re-occurring musical interjection is Selah, 71 times in the Psalter, predominantly in Books 1–3. It likely denotes a pause or musical interlude. The Aramaic verb 'to bend' infers a bowing down before the LORD to reflect upon what had been said or sung in the Psalm. In the Mishnah's description of the singing of the daily psalm, trumpets were blown in between the three parts, fitting with when Selah was used. The people responded by prostrating themselves.[6] A closely linked term is *Higgaion* (used in Psalms 9, 19 and

---

5. Henry, *Matthew Henry's Online Bible Commentary*.

6. Eerdmans, *Hebrew Book of Psalms*, 85.

92) meaning 'to murmur' or meditate within the heart, thus, the deduction can be made for quiet music or a pause to reflect.

Further terms include: *Miktan* from the transliterated term which may refer to gold, atonement—'a covering' or pillar of inscription. *Miktam* (used in Psalms 16, 56–60) may be used to highlight an intimate, secret, silent prayer, hence the name *Katamu* 'to cover.'[7] *Maschil / Maskil* (Psalms 32, 42, 44, 45, 52–55, 74, 78, 88, 89, 142), derived from the verb to be 'skilled' or 'wise'. These psalms are instructional, designed to impart wisdom to the reader. *Shiggaion* is a lamentation occurring once in the Psalter, as in the inscription of Psalm 7, from the verb to 'err' or 'wander'. However, Psalm 7 is not penitential by nature and *Shiggaion* eludes easy definition. *Tehillah* means 'song of praise'-*shir tehillah*—where the Psalmist expresses thanks and praise to God. *Tefillah* or 'prayer' is a noun occurring in five psalms (17, 86, 90, 102 and 142). The references usually are imploring God to forgive, work in hearts and in the nations bringing people to repentance and faith.

Some psalms have specific titles which highlight something of their nature or how they are to be played. *Lamenatstseakh* (to the choir master) is noted 55 times which is from the verb 'to lead' or 'excel', indicating superintendence. *Binginoth* and '*al-neginoth*' refer to psalms with stringed accompaniment, occurring in six of the psalms. This is derived from the verb 'to run over the strings.' 'Upon the Neginah' refers to stringed instruments and 'Upon Nehioloth' to wind instruments. '*Al-hashinith*' ('according to the eighth') suggests that the instruments are tuned for bass singers. Al'al-muth, 'almuth labben and '*al-alamoth*' means 'according to maidens' with instruments tuned for the maidens or virgins with their voices as sopranos and the bass tuned an octave lower (Reformation Heritage Study Bible). 'According to *Gittith*' (Psalms 8, 81, 84) refers to Gath the Philistine town, from which the instruments played may have come or a wine press, which the name may suggest. Finally, 'According to *Muthlabben*' (only occurring in Psalm 9) 'upon the death (*muth*) of a son or fool (*labben*)' or 'secrets of a son' assigned to the chief musician or choir master. This may have been David's

---

7. Kidner, *Psalms 1–72*, 53.

lament over Absalom's death (2 Samuel 18:33) or used of a musical instrument or as a type of musical tune. This work explores now the interpretive methodological approaches taken in interpreting psalms in general, and then specifically Psalm 119.

AUTHORSHIP OF PSALMS

It is important to interpret psalms after ascertaining who the author was wherever possible. Of equal importance is deducing the literary style and purpose of the writing, as each will be framed within a context. The methodological tool of exploring the context and content of any account is key to successful analysis.[8] For example, the Davidic Psalms, the largest number, across the Books (as defined above), portray David as a shepherd, a harpist, a victim, a victor, a sinner, a child of God who knew how to touch God in prayer, a king and so forth. Specifically, Psalm 86 highlights how David had a prayerful life and was a devoted servant of God, and prays affirming the LORD as his God 'you are my God' (verse 2). He wanted to learn God's way and live according to His Word; David recognised his need of God and trusted Him to save him. Verse 11 notes his prayer for dependency as he asks God to 'teach him His way'. He recognised God's mercy, love and patience and the help he had received and was full of praise to God and gave Him the glory, expressing 'how great is your mercy toward me' (verse 13).

Further works of David are the Michtam Psalms (16, 56–60), written as 'golden Psalms', engraved as testimonies of pertinent events. All of these salms, in the inscription, have to be the 'chief musician', in charge of the choir (except Psalm 16, which is a personal reflective praise). From this we recognise that these Psalms were meant for public singing and memorisation. Also, 'Al-taschith' or 'do not destroy' follows, as a reminder to retain these truths, as a preserved testimony of memorial. Michtam Psalms were written at a time when David was fleeing from persecution. Psalm 16:1 David asks for God's preservation, sentiments echoed in Psalm 56:1, where David expresses how man would seek to eat him up. Yet, in

---

8. Erben, *Biography and Education: A Reader*, 8.

all of these within this genre, David writes from the perspective of one who is wholly trusting in God. He knows God has the resources and power to execute His will. Some of the Michtam psalms have tones of imprecation (an appeal to God to judge the unrepentant). For example, in Psalm 58 David prays for God to judge those who are like 'deaf adders'. They are illustrative of heedless individuals who won't listen to God's will (verse 4). Further, he prays God would disarm the lions, whose sins are like the strength of lion teeth seeking to destroy him (verse 6). He prays God would stop the floods of the ungodly, destroy their weapons and dissolve their plans like the snail reduced to slime. David knows that God can discontinue the pregnancy (of a godless seed) and disrupt their cooking (of pernicious schemes), with a gust of wind (verses 7–9).

The sons of Korah, writers of Psalms 42, 49, 84–85 and 87 were connected to the 'Korahites', 'Korathites', 'Korhites' and 'sons of Kore'. Korah was the great-grandson of Levi who led a Levitical rebellion against Moses and Aaron. Numbers 16:2 records how they defiantly mobilised forces against God's appointed leadership: 'And they rose up before Moses . . .'. They suggested the leadership was arrogated and sought, unlawfully, to perform the work of priests (indicating defiance against the mediation of God). Consequently, they were swallowed up in the earth and a further plague broke out destroying many lives. However, his sons, ko'-ra-its (*qorchi*), were spared (Numbers 26:11). Later, in the scriptures, the Korahites were supportive of David and are named among the helpers of war in 1 Chronicles 12.

A feature of the Korah Psalms is the use of the expression *Elohim* (God) in Psalms 42 to 49 and the predominant usage of *Yahweh* / Jehovah (LORD) in Psalms 84–85 and 87. This signifies a high view of God's holiness; perhaps God's dealings with those who defied His name, had sealed a greater reverence in their minds for His holy worship and authority?

Despite God's purity, these psalms often indicate a desire to know God in a deeper relational way. For example, expressions of this can be found in Psalm 42:1, 'As the hart panteth after the water brooks, so my soul after thee, O God.' Equally, in Psalm 84:2, 'My soul longeth, yea, even fainteth for the courts of the LORD; my heart and flesh cry out for the living God.'

The next category of Psalms concerns Asaph, a significant Levite singer in David's court and the ancestor of the Sons of Asaph (temple musicians). He was the chief of the Levites to minister before the Ark of The Lord (1 Chronicles 6; 15;16; 2 Chronicles 29). The Psalms of Asaph, 50, 73–83, are a collection of psalms concerned predominantly with Israel's enemies and how God would deal with them. Psalm 50, for example, notes the distinguishing differences between the godly and the ungodly whom, if they remained unrepentant, God would judge and they would not be spared.[9] Strikingly, verse 22 states: 'Now consider this, ye who forget God, lest I tear *you* in pieces, and *there be* none to deliver'. Equally, in Psalm 74 we learn that Israel's enemies have brought destruction on the sanctuary (the place of solace / refuge). Correspondingly, Psalm 76 describes with acclamation that the LORD crushes His enemies and thus He is to be reverenced by all, including leaders: 'Thou didst cause judgment to be heard from heaven; the earth feared, and was still' (v.8).

Last, in this section, the Songs of Degrees (or Ascents), the chapters 120–34. Cox describes these psalms: 'It is a little gem, cut with the most exquisite art.'[10] The English verb 'to go up' is thought to relate to the annual journey to Jerusalem at the time of Passover and the feast of unleavened bread, and the other feasts to the Lord (Leviticus 23). The participants would have sung the psalms as they went to the festival / feast. It is also quite probable that the Levites sang these songs as they stood on the steps of the temple. These Pilgrim Psalms are said to have been sung going up to Zion (1 Samuel 1:3; Psalm 122:4; Zechariah 14:19). Many psalms within this group of Songs of Ascent have attributed titles: Psalm 122, 124, 131 and 133 are of David, Psalm 127 bears Solomon's name. The other songs (Psalm 120, 121, 123, 125, 126, 128, 129, 130, 132 and 134) are anonymous.

9. Zorn, *College Press NIV Commentary*, 40.
10. Cox, *Pilgrim Psalms*, 69.

THE TYPES AND PURPOSES OF THE PSALMS

The psalms are chiefly expressions of praise to God. The Hebrew 'hallelu' refers to praise and 'yau', the abbreviated version of Yahweh, thus, praise the LORD. Bullock writes: 'A case can be made on the basis of the salms that the purpose of human existence is to praise God.'[11] The Psalmist gives a clarion call, '*Let* the high praises of God *be* in their mouth and a two-edged sword in their hand' (Psalm 149:6). The specific Hallelujah Psalms are Psalm 106, 111–113, 135 and 146–150. For example, 'Praise God or the LORD' occurs 12 times in Psalm 150. The Reformation Heritage Study Bible argues this could be the 12 tribes and 12 Apostles.[12] Our praise to God is that He may graciously interact with mere mankind, how gracious is the condescension of God. The importance of rousing ourselves to praise God is significant as our day-to-day experiences can hinder our responsiveness to give God glory in thankfulness. Normally, the Psalms directly seek to praise God who is 'sitting' or 'inhabiting' the praises of Israel (Psalm 22:3). In so doing, reading, singing, meditating upon them may spark desire for heartfelt praise to God. Moreover, Psalm 106:1 notes –'Praise ye the Lord. O give thanks unto the Lord; for He is good: for his mercy endures for ever.'

Psalms of thanksgiving (*todah*) come from the verb 'yadah' meaning to 'thank'. Thanksgiving Psalms include Psalms 18, 30, 31, 32, 40, 66, 92, 116, 118 and 120. In each of these examples a report is given of the situation or a problem, the deliverance is described and the reason for the deliverance is echoed. For example, Psalm 18 affirms God as his strength as he notes how the cords of death strangle and overwhelm him, there is hostility of enemies around about. Next, the deliverance occurs as prayer is made, God intervenes in the nation or particular situation: 'The LORD also thundered in the heavens, and the Highest gave his voice; hail *stones* and coals of fire.' (Psalm 18:13). Finally, the sentiments are perpetually echoed that God has wrought such a deliverance because of His mercy and love. A community of Psalms which praise God are within the canon of scripture. Moreover, Psalm 118, for instance, reports on

---

11. Bullock, *Encountering the Book of Psalms*, 122.

12. *Reformation Heritage Study Bible*. Reformation Heritage, 757.

Israel's warfare and encourages the community in thanksgiving: 'O give thanks unto the LORD; for *He is* good: because his mercy *endureth* for ever' (v. 1). This thanksgiving is an iterative feature of the Psalms cited above and resounds from hearts which are thankful for God's salvation, borne out of devotional love to Him. The six specific Hallel Psalms (numbers 113–18) were used on festive occasions, including at the Passover before and after partaking of the lamb feast. They underscore God's mercy (Psalm 113), redemption (Psalm 114), the requirement of faith (Psalm 115), and eternal life secured and universally offered in the gospel call (Psalms 116–17).

Psalms which emphasise trust in God include Psalm 4, Psalm 16, Psalm 23, Psalm 27, Psalm 62, Psalm 73, Psalm 90, and Psalms 123–26. Psalm 4, for example, records how He will commune with JEHOVAH as He alone is His safety; 'for thou, Lord, only makest me dwell in safety' (v.8). This Psalm emphasises the trust the writer has in the true God and how this led him to praise Him (as his inner man was strengthened) and culminated in the joy of peace and protection. These sentiments are echoed in the well-known Psalm 23. However, a golden thread which runs through Psalm 32, for example, is when things are not as they should be then joy is not apparent and peace is forfeited until the relationship is restored by repentance as the blood of Christ washes over us. A further example of God's contingent protection (based upon a right standing with Him) is shown in Psalm 27, where the writer is assured of God's safe keeping, hidden in the shadow of his shelter and tabernacle. A parallel exists with Bunyan's allegory, the Pilgrim's Progress, when Christian on the way towards the Celestial City comes to the valley of the shadow of death. Some retreat but Christian boldly presses towards the glory.[13]

Psalm 73 accentuates the goodness of God in a clear affirmation; 'Truly God is good to Israel, even to such as are of a clean heart' (verse 1). Next, he affirms his inner battles but looks towards eternity and revisits the goodness of the LORD with a renewed perspective. This is a lesson for us all not to be consumed with this life but to look, with the eye of faith, at eternal matters. Asaph finds a 'solution

13. Bunyan, *Pilgrim's Progress*, 58.

in the sanctuary,' teaching the importance of being in the House of God and ever in prayer.[14] Psalm 90 deals with the calming of the soul, likely penned by Moses as a clear marker of God's abiding presence with His people. Last, Psalms 123–126 each use remembrance of God and His attributes to remind us of their trust in Him and confidence for the future. For example, Psalm 125:1–2 states:

> They that trust in the Lord shall be as mount Zion, which cannot be removed, but abideth forever. As the mountains are round about Jerusalem, so the Lord is round about his people from henceforth even forever.

The importance of admiration of nature is underscored in some of the Psalms. These are known as nature Psalms. In so doing, this category of Psalms underlines the greatness of God as creator of all things and admires His handiwork. The rationale of these Psalms is to drive the reader to praise God and appreciate Him more as one views the awesomeness of His creation. Jesse Reeves is said to have inspired Chris Tomlin, contemporary song writer, to write the following lyrics as he reflected upon some of these aspects of nature.[15]

The nature psalms are: Psalms 8, (19 also known along with Psalm 119 as a Word Psalm), 29, 104 and 147. Jesus references a nature type Psalm in expressing common grace in nature: Matthew 5:45, 'He makes the sun to shine upon the just and unjust. . .' God works for man's benefit through all He has created through Christ and abides with His presence in the universe. He takes a present active involvement in the lives of human beings, working miraculously and in providence (Colossians 1:17). To select one example, in Psalm 8 God's excellent name is witnessed by the creation. The Psalm opens noting the personal relationship David has with his God, the One whose name is 'expansive' (the translation of 'excellent'): 'O LORD our Lord how excellent is thy name in all the earth who hast set thy glory above the heavens' (v.1). As David looks back to his youth, being a shepherd, under the night canopy, it is likely that he reflects upon the heavens, the direct result of God's conscious creation. To see the beauty of creation is to see something of

14. Bullock, *Encountering the Book of Psalms*, 173.

15. Tomlin, "*Indescribable.*"

the greatness of God; Nahum 1:3 states that the clouds are likened to 'the dust of His feet'. This is humbling as it shows how small and insignificant human beings are compared to the great God yet God takes thought and cares for us (Psalm 8:4). Synthetic parallelism is used as David in Psalm 8 builds upon how God is in charge of the animals, the elements and all things—in so doing, he builds up a picture of an all-powerful God. The symmetry of the poetry of Psalm 8 is structured as follows: the Psalm begins with praise verses 1 and 2, then creation verse 3, man verses 4–8 and concludes with praise verse 9.

Word Psalms, specifically Psalms 19 and 119, are about God's Word. Their rationale is to praise God for His universal and special revelation to us. There are overlaps between Psalms 19 and 119, this work addresses the specific points of Psalm 119 in detail. Thus, this section briefly mentions Psalm 19, which uses the nuanced terms for the scriptures and highlights the importance and value and purpose of each:

- Law—perfect—restores
- Testimony—sure—gives wisdom
- Precepts—right—making the heart rejoice
- Commandments—pure—enlightenment
- Fear—clean—assurance
- Judgments—true / righteous, precious and pleasing-protection.

The general revelation of God is seen in the speechless skies, yet they make a deep impression. Verse 1 states: 'The heavens declare the glory of God and the firmament sheweth his handiwork'. The root of 'glory' is weight or heavy which testify of the creator. However, the special revelation of God is seen in the Torah of Yahweh is 'perfect' (v.7). The 'testimony' of case histories and experiences are 'sure' in witnessing a child-like faith to the hearer or reader. Consequently, David says he is desirous of the Word 'more than fine gold' (v.10). The scriptures are more desirable than the greatest gold (the wealth of the world) and more nourishing than the purest and sweetest honey (the pleasure of the senses). It warns the wicked not to continue his downward way and warns the righteous not to turn from God's perfect way. There is a reward for patient endurance of a life lived in accordance with God's Word.

Next, Messianic Psalms describe the Messiah (the 'anointed One'), referring to Israel's true king and ultimate fulfilment of scripture. Below, in Table 1.1, there is a compilation of the clearest Messianic Psalms and the salient fulfilments in the New Testament.

Table 1.1. Messianic Psalms and Scriptural fulfilments.

Incarnation	Ministry	Trials	Crucifixion	Resurrection	Ascension	Futuristic
Psalm 2:7	Psalm 40:7–8	Psalm 35:11, 19	Psalm 22:1,7–8, 16–18	Psalm 16:10	Psalm 68:18	Psalm 2:6
Psalm 8:2	Psalm 69:9	Psalm 41:9	Psalm 31:5		Psalm 118:22	Psalm 8:6
	Psalm 78:2–4		Psalm 34:20			Psalm 45:6–7
			Psalm 69:21			Psalm 110:1
						Psalm 110:4

Psalm 8:2 in Matthew 21:6 (you have taught the little ones to praise)	Psalm 69:9 (passion for your house consumed me) in John 2:17 Psalms 118:25–26 (blessed be the one who comes in the name of the Lord) in Matthew 21:9, 23:39, Mark 11:10, Luke 13:35, 19:38 and John 12:13. Psalm 91:11–12 (angels ordered to protect you) in Matthew 4:6 and Luke 4:10–11	Psalm 35:11 (hostile witnesses lie and hate without reason) in John 15:21. Psalm 41:9 (lifted heel against me) in John 13:18	Psalm 22:18 (dividing garments) Matthew 27:35, Mark 15:24, Luke 23:34 and John 19:24. Psalm 69:21 (offering sour wine for thirst) in John 19:28 Psalm 22:1 (God, why have you forsaken me) in Matthew 27:46.	Psalm 16:10 (not leave soul in grave—resurrection accounts, Matthew 28, Mark 16, Luke 24 and John 20; Acts 2:27	Luke 24:50–53 (led the disciples to Bethany and blessed them and ascended to heaven)	

Psalm 31:5 (Commit my spirit to you) in Luke 23:46; Psalm 35:19 (not let treacherous enemies gloat) in John 15:25 Psalm 34:20 (Lord protects the bones of the righteous, they will not be broken) in John 19:36	Psalm 110:1 (sit in the place until I make your enemies a footstall) in Matthew 22:44, 26:64, Mark 12:36, 14:62 and Luke 20:43, 22:69 Psalm 118:22–23 (the stone the builders reject becomes the chief cornerstone) in Matthew 21:42, Mark 12:10 and Luke 20:17 Psalm 78:2 (I speak in parables) in Matthew 13:35 Psalm 78:24 (given Bread from Heaven) in John 6:31

To isolate a few examples, Psalm 2, for instance, describes the Lord's Messiah as His Son, clearly not David but one far greater than David. Specifically, these references are typological of an eternal one, Jesus (Son of God), to whom all should pay homage. 'Kiss the Son' (v.12), is employed as an expression of honour and to denote submission due to the Messiah. The passion of Christ is most clearly prophesied in Psalm 22. As a result of His substitutionary atonement, a seed of believers would 'serve him' (v.30). Such language depicts one who would rule hearts and lives. Jesus was able to accomplish salvation for His people on account of being the God-man. Christ's preeminence and authoritative nature is encapsulated in the Greek *prototokos* ('firstborn'). Colossians 1:15, notes, 'Who is the image of the invisible God, the firstborn of every creature.' Psalm 45 notes the Kingship of Jesus and has it re-emphasised in Hebrews 1, equally, Psalm 110 states Christ's role—the Lord of David and High Priest (Hebrews 5). Lieth notes how a number of Psalms have clear Messianic implications, such as Psalm 8: 5, 6:

> For thou hast made him a little lower than the angels, and
> hast crowned him with glory and honour. Thou madest
> him to have dominion over the works of thy hands; thou
> hast put all things under his feet.[16]

Such verses, according to Leith, emphasise the lowliness of man, the greatness of God and yet, He would come incarnate. To summarise, Keller notes, '. . . there are a number of very obvious Messianic Psalms that give us a particular view of Christ.'[17] These include: the enthroned Jesus (Psalms 2 and 10), the rejected Messiah (Psalm 118), the betrayed Christ (Psalms 69 and 109), the dying and risen Saviour (Psalms 22 and 16), the heavenly bridegroom of His people (Psalm 45) and the triumphant Messiah (Psalms 68 and 72).

The Royal Psalms are eschatologically prophetic within Kingship theology and have referent to David and David's ancestral line, the ultimate ruler, the Messiah. They take a high view of soteriology and Christology, penned to honour the majesty and wonder of God, who He is and what He has done, telescoping specific

16. Lieth, *Messianic Psalms*, 32.
17. Keller, *Prayer*, 258.

events—noting God's immutability—thus able to act now as He did in the past. The noun Messiah, meaning 'Anointed One' has historical and eschatological references—the King of Israel and the Greater David, pointing to the King, who is Christ. Psalm 45, for example, is layered: first as historicity (Solomon and princesses), metaphorically (God and the nation) and lastly, Messianic (God and the church). The Psalm can be interpreted in different layers as a marriage about to take place, Solomon and the Egyptian princess—a wedding, a relationship produced. First, the bride is admired and the beauty of being together and being forever the bride of the king—this is similar to the Song of Solomon. However, the marriage denotes a higher relationship, that of the relationship between Christ and His people. The church should not let the past define them, should submit to her husband (Jesus), purified and made ready to be wed to the King. Finally, on another level, a higher and sublime, a poignant picture is painted, the psalm records how Jesus relates to His church by His atonement. It further denotes how knowing Him creates a future royal heritage, who will reign with Him forever.

Another example of this type of Psalm can be seen in Psalm 110:1–4:

> The Lord said unto my Lord, Sit thou at my right hand, until I make thine enemies thy footstool. The Lord shall send the rod of thy strength out of Zion: rule thou in the midst of thine enemies. Thy people shall be willing in the day of thy power, in the beauties of holiness from the womb of the morning: thou hast the dew of thy youth. The Lord hath sworn, and will not repent, Thou art a priest for ever after the order of Melchizedek.

This is the priest-king relationship. It is the most quoted psalm in the New Testament. Some of the statements can be applied to David yet most of them can only be applied to Christ—the ideal King and Messiah. The salm begins with, 'The Lord says to my lord. . .' Jesus notes in Matthew 22:44–46 that David was not simply referring to himself but to the future divine Messiah, whose army and rule was vastly superior. Jesus Himself quotes from this psalm to elicit from those around Him that He indeed was the Messiah (Mark 12:35–37). The same king is also anointed as a priest (Psalm 110:4), which is only fulfilled in the future application of Jesus, as kings did not serve as priests and who could claim universality and eternity but a divine being (typified in Melchizedek)? In so doing, the one prophesied would exercise sovereign rulership and judgment over all the nations, verse 5–7. Again, the kings which are recorded in scripture exercised localised authority of a region, but none but Christ could fulfil this commission. In summary, Arnold and Beyer state:

> Royal Psalms focus on Israel's king. They usually describe him as God's special representative to rule Israel. The Lord would accomplish his purpose through his anointed servant. They also sometimes portray him as the heir to God's covenant with David (2 Samuel 7). His faithfulness would bring God's blessing forever.[18]

Jesus is ultimately the eternal king. John 8:58 records how Jesus spoke His eternal name, Yahweh, 'I am'. By using a present tense verb—the tetragrammaton—He was claiming deity. Equally, Christ is the eternal king, whose scepter is over all (Hebrews 1:8). Finally, in Revelation Jesus is the soon coming king above all kings (Revelation 19:6). Wisdom Psalms (specifically 1, 37, 49, 112 and 127) are didactic, normally short summaries of experience and common wisdom, designed to teach the reader in a practical way. Wisdom also occurs in the books of Proverbs, Job, Song of Songs and Ecclesiastes. They emphasise the sovereignty of God and the characteristics of a righteous person. In addition, they teach the importance of true temple worship, the blessedness of bearing fruit for the LORD and the overall importance of the value of seeking heavenly wisdom and obedience. The importance of getting wisdom 'Hakam', and related terms, appear more than 300 times in the Old Testament. Hakam means to live life skilfully; wisdom is living life consistent with God's will and covenants. This category of psalms provides instructional teaching (see Psalms 1, 14, 25, 34, 37, 39, 49, 73, 78, 90, 91, 111, 112, 127, 128, 131, 133, 139). Many

18. Arnold and Beyer, *Encountering the Old Testament*, 285.

other psalms contain elements of wisdom teaching (such as Psalms 18, 27, 31, 32, 40, 62, 92, 94, 107, 144, 146).

Psalm 1, for example, stresses the importance of godly wisdom, bearing fruit for the LORD at all seasons of life by being planted in God's house doing His will / obeying and meditating upon the scriptures. Psalm 14 deals with atheism or questions about God, noting the folly of having an entrenched position against the LORD. By contrast, filial fear of God brings the wisdom and opens our hearts and mouths as our soul praises the LORD (Psalm 34). The psalm reminds us of a comforting but fearful fact, the God watches over His people but has regard for those who love Him in sincerity.

Within wisdom Psalms these can be divided into three sub-types:

- Experience (Marshals, *Maskil*) or proverbial psalms such as Psalm 78, where specific teaching is given and each point works towards a climax. Another example is Psalm 133, stating ceremonial anointing to highlight the blessing of scriptural unity (emblematic parallelism).

- Character Psalms answer the question: how should a person live before God? Psalm 1, the threshold Psalm, contrasts two ways of life (synonymous parallelism): how to be godly contrasted to the ungodly. Thus, it highlights how to avoid certain things and embrace other things to build up the character of godliness, his nourishment is the Word of God. A further example, is Psalm 15: who can come to God? The question is answered in both positive (integrity, a way of life, acts according to God's will, not a hypocrite) and negative form (not slander, do evil or distress others about what they have done)

- Ethical Psalms deal with ethics and religion: dilemmas such as: if God is sovereign why do the wicked seem to prosper and escape penalties? Yet, the righteous suffer and appear to be denied happiness and prosperity. Psalm 49 deals with the pertinent issue, wealth cannot buy God off when death comes. Death is the great equaliser; the grave is the ultimate end to life here below and things of pomp will be as nought. Redemption is embedded within Messianic promises: God will save the humble sinner who repents and trusts in Him, which is the ultimate reversal of those who congratulate themselves in this life but will have no eternal blessing.

Penitential Psalms (or lament) reflect upon the consequences of sin—in particular, the estrangement from the felt presence of God. For example, the writer of Psalm 6, pleads with God when he is suffering and asks for a reprieve from the punishment he feels chastised by. In the belief, that he is dying, he pleads: who shall praise you if I die when you are angry at me? (Psalm 6:4,5). Psalm 143 is a reflection upon the good times when David felt blessed but now feels estranged from God and his enemies are gaining a victory. Thus, David knew this should not be the case and asks God for renewed vitality by means of repentance and renewed deliverance from the adversary. These psalms involve confession—asking for forgiveness of sins, admitting wrongdoing and seeking pardon and reconciliation with God. Often the term 'steadfast love' (*hesed*), also translated mercy, lovingkindness, goodness, is used within these laments. This denotes God's immutable covenantal love, despite our unworthiness and sinfulness.

Within this category of Psalms those commonly thought to be penitential are: 6, 32, 38, 51, 102, 130, 143. The most well-known psalm within this category is psalm 51, where David confesses his sin of sexual relations with Bathsheba and the aftermath of this, inclusive of covering his sinful guilt as an initial response. This psalm pleads with God for a thorough washing inside and out, to extend mercy to David, despite his sexual sin and murderous plot of her husband (Uriah) in battle (2 Samuel 11). David asks God to stop him at the point of temptation, not to revel in it and play with sin, which has a cumulative, domino effect. He also recognises in personal pronouns, I and my; acknowledging his sins and not making excuses for them is key to reconciliation. The use of synonymous terms noting the need of forgiveness are used throughout: 'blot out' (v.1), 'wash me' (v.2), 'cleanse me' (v.2), 'purify me' (v.7), 'hide' (v.9), 'create a clean heart' (v.10), 'do not cast me out' (v.11), 'restore me' (v.12) and 'deliver me' (v.14). David is acutely aware of how sin causes a barrier between him and God, the withdrawal of His presence and, the grieving of the Spirit. Verse 11 notes: 'Do not cast me away from Your presence, and do not take Your Holy Spirit from me.' Consequently, he implores the LORD to act for him, sending his Spirit again and bringing him back into fellowship. The penitential Psalms feel the weight of sin (verses 3 and 4):

> For I acknowledge my transgressions, And my sin *is* always before me. Against You, You only, have I sinned, And done *this* evil in Your sight, That You may be found just when You speak, *And* blameless when You judge.

David notes how his behaviour is primarily against God and he deserves God's justice but instead, pleads for mercy. His sins included lust, adultery, guilt of sin, pre-meditated murder and concealing his sins. David desires a new and responsive heart to God's ways and thus to perform them with sincere desire and enthusiasm.[19]

Penitential pleas include those praying for a new, clean heart devoted to God, asking for pardoning grace, accompanied with sincere entreaties: 'Cause me to know the way wherein I should walk, Teach me to do Thy will' (Psalm 143:8–10). This is salient in the Psalm as it is why David sinned—his heart was not fully right at this point in his life. Sinful associations also are renounced as the workers of iniquity are bidden to depart (Psalm 6:8). Finally, David notes the importance of right communion as being a poor witness can have implications upon the gospel. Sin shuts one's mouth as the individual who engages in wilful or secret sin cannot testify effectively and openly to others of the grace of God and how Christ has saved them from the power of sin. Verse 13 of Psalm 51 states: '*Then* I will teach transgressors Your ways and sinners shall be converted to You'. The testimony of David's sin caused open damage to God's work, as the enemies of God blasphemed. Zion's work is impacted when we sin, as our behaviour affects others; when right with God we have a restored prayer life where we desire to pray for others and the work of the kingdom—and God hears and answers: 'Do good in Your good pleasure to Zion; Build the walls of Jerusalem' (verse 18). If unrepentant, God will choose not to hear us, Psalm 66:18 and God hides by clothing Himself from us like a cloud that our prayers

19. Keeys, *Step by Step: The Big Picture Chapter by Chapter*, 231.

are not answered. Lamentation 3:44 writes: 'You have covered Your-self with a cloud, that prayer should not pass through.' How we need to keep in check these things as our testimony needs to be as bright lights in a dark day. The joy of knowing all is well between you and God is also linked with communion with Him, as David in verse 12 of Psalm 51 prays for joy to return after confession is made and pardon granted—a specific theme also of Psalm 32. This psalm re-tells David's restoration after he vows to spend his life telling others of God's salvation (Psalm 51:13). He begins by proclaiming the blessedness (happiness) of forgiveness (Psalm 32:1–2). The condition of forgiveness is contingent upon true repentance of wilful, stubborn sin. Without it, he was ill, wasting away, depressed (Psalm 32:3,4). Only by openly confessing sins, was he forgiven and the judgment of God was then lifted from his life (Psalm 32:5).

Finally, imprecatory Psalms (notably Psalms 69 and 109) are those such as, 'May they be blotted out of the Book of Life and not listed with the righteous' (Psalm 69:28). Another remarks:

> Let there be none to extend mercy unto him: neither let there be any to favour his fatherless children. Let his posterity be cut off; and in the generation following let their name be blotted out. (Psalm 109:12, 13).

The term 'imprecatory' means 'curses', praying evil against or a curse upon a person or nation. There are imprecations in other Psalms such as: Psalms 5, 6, 11, 12, 35, 37, 40, 52, 54, 56, 57, 58, 59, 79, 83, 94, 137, 139, and 143 but Psalms 69 and 109 are explicitly of this type. In these, the Psalmist is seeking God for curses to be placed upon his personal enemies and those of God and His kingdom. A superficial reading of this genre of Psalms supposes it to be a bloodthirsty category of literature. However, this creates moral and ethical problems. Some have suggested that the imprecations are spiritual, hyperboles or poetical.[20] Yet, a fair interpretation of this cannot, in the writer's view, lead one to such a conclusion, as the reading of them necessitates that the Psalmist is vexed by his enemies and cries to God to vindicate and to exercise His vengeance.

20. Rogerson & McKay, *The Cambridge Bible Commentary on the New English Bible: Psalms 51–100*, 97.

There appear to be principles in these types of Psalms, prayers which may be offered in such cases may be for national deliverance, protection from slander / false accusation or for restoration. Indeed, The Old Testament is not alone in containing imprecations. Jesus taught we should pray for those who persecute us (Matthew 5:44). Equally, He denounced hypocrisy:

- Matthew 23:13 'But woe unto you, scribes and Pharisees, hypocrites! for ye shut up the kingdom of heaven against men: for ye neither go in yourselves, neither suffer ye them that are entering to go in.'

- Matthew 26:23–24 'And He answered and said, He that dippeth his hand with me in the dish, the same shall betray me. 24 The Son of man goeth as it is written of him: but woe unto that man by whom the Son of man is betrayed! it had been good for that man if he had not been born.'

The Apostle Paul wrote as warnings:

- 1 Corinthians 16:22 'If any man love not the Lord Jesus Christ, let him be Anathema Maranatha.'

- Galatians 1:8–9 'But though we, or an angel from heaven, preach any other gospel unto you than that which we have preached unto you, let him be accursed. 9 As we said before, so say I now again, If any man preach any other gospel unto you than that ye have received, let him be accursed.'

- Galatians 5:12 'I would they were even cut off which trouble you.'

- 2 Timothy 4:14 'Alexander the coppersmith did me much evil: the Lord reward him according to his works'

Finally, John records in Revelation 6:10, 'And they cried with a loud voice, saying, How long, O Lord, holy and true, dost thou not judge and avenge our blood on them that dwell on the earth?'

In summary, the psalms offer divinely inspired perspectives of lives experiences., offering insights into personal prayers as well as communal praise.[21] They are rich in theology, exalting God, noting His acts in nature and providence. Some, such as the Messianic ones, specifically point to Jesus, the Messiah. The psalms are rather like a treasure chest within a book like none other.

21. Brown, *The Oxford Handbook of Psalms*, 3.

CHAPTER 2

A devotional exposition
of Psalm 119

THIS CHAPTER IS THE study of the Psalm 119 itself, analysing literary features and the notion of holiness through exposition. In so doing it examines each of the 22 stanzas of the Hebrew alphabet and draws pertinent points from the verses, seeking to give application to the points raised. This chapter can be used as a 22-day study, pausing at each section for prayerful reflection about what the Psalm says for that day.

THE STUDY OF THE PSALM

Psalm Chapter 119 תְּהִלִּים

This Psalm is an autobiographical account of the Psalmist explaining what it is like to follow the LORD, adhere to His Word and the impact / consequences of choosing such a life. Unlike man-centred theological narratives, Psalm 119 is chiefly about God. In so doing, the writer reflects upon God and His word, rather like the meditations of Nathanael in John 1:48. Withal, 'Meditations on the excellence of the Word of God' to aptly describe the beauty of the Psalm.[1]

---

1. MacArthur, *MacArthur Study Bible*, 850.

The verses of Psalm 119 progressively flow, building and cementing themes, rather than haphazard thoughts of walking in the way of the Word. The literary tools used, guided by the Spirit, are purposeful, ordered, progressive and convey completeness.[2] First, the heading ALEPH refers to God the Father, the Master and the Truth (the Lord Jesus Christ). To begin, verse one notes the blessedness, supreme happiness, unsurprising joy of knowing God in a relational way and being 'undefiled' (complete or sound) in the way. This is not sinless perfection, rather a heart and life aligned with their profession—of being a Christian.[3] Happiness is found in loving the Word of God. This involves practically living out the principles of the Torah.[4] This is a reminder of the Beatitudes expressed by the Lord Jesus Christ in the Sermon on the Mount (Matthew 5; Luke 6). Thus, the 'poor in spirit' (Matthew 5:3) is the one who has recognised the desperate plight they are in, is in distress and spiritual poverty / bankruptcy as they stand before God. On account of this they mourn over their sin which has made them poor; there is a paradox of being happy if you mourn, as the pathway of repentance leads one to weep over sins by the conviction of the Holy Spirit. These are the entry terms into the kingdom of God.

א. אַשְׁרֵי תְמִימֵי-דָרֶךְ—הַהֹלְכִים, בְּתוֹרַת יְהוָה	1 ALEPH. Blessed are the undefiled, who walk in the law of the LORD.

Aleph, the heading of this section of the psalm, refers to 'truth', being truthful with God about how great He is and how miniature we are in comparison The happiness of the one who seeks to keep all of God's commands is accentuated in verse two: 'Testimonies', divine witness of truth, mark the acts of God within scripture or solemn declarations. The testimony of men can be flawed, inaccurate and unreliable but God's is about His Son; whoever believes in the Son has life within them (1 John 5:9). This belief leads to obedience. They 'crave' obedience to the revealed Word, as the Amplified

2. Isom, *Walk with the Word*, Psalm 119, 9.

3. Poole, *Matthew Poole's Commentary*, Psalm 119.

4. Chapman, *Thy Word*, 3.

version states. The importance of loving God with the 'whole heart' (verse 2, of Psalm 119) is clearly taught as an important aspect of sincerity to approaching God's Word. Holiness necessitates whole-heartedness to the revealed will of God. This is expressed in the greatest commandments, Matthew 22:36–40 outlines our love for the LORD and others should be unrivalled.In verse 1 of Psalm 119, the 'undefiled', does not refer to flawless perfection in Hebrew. If this were the case, it would leave everyone utterly condemned, as no human could attain to such a standard. Rather it means sound, complete, or one, like Job, who possessed sincerity and integrity (Job 1:1). Jesus said that the Father's commandments were eternal life (John 12:50). The 'heart' refers to intellect, disposition and emotion, the 'whole heart' occurs six times (verses 2, 10, 34, 58, 69 and 145) relating to passionate desire or commitment to obey.[5]

The next verse of this psalm, verse 3, examines the estate in which the child of God is not a habitual wilful sinner; they cannot intentionally sin or plan to sin in a pre-meditated way By adhering to the scriptures, holiness is developed. Cole uses two terms 'current reality' and 'transformed reality' to depict how Christ changes behaviour.[6] Sin should grieve the Christian and cause them to hate it as it hinders the blessedness of communing with God. The importance of not letting sin reign within and walking in God's paths is taught in this verse. The Amplified version comments: 'no wilful wanderings from His precepts'. This is because the Psalmist loves the LORD, and as verse four notes, as the author of these commands is God—disobedience creates alienation and sorrow, whereas obedience is an expression of love. The 'iniquity' mentioned here as also in the Maschil (of instruction) Psalm 32 where 'sin', 'iniquity' and 'transgression' (verse) are used is the pre-meditated, deep-rooted perversions, contrasted to 'transgressions', referring to law breaking (i.e. God's law), wickedness, going over the mark of what is right. Finally, the word 'sin' (Psalm 32:1) is referent to missing the mark / standard of a holy God, the bent, twistedness creates a negative result. The only happiness is when all of this lawlessness is 'covered'

5. Bullock, *Encountering the Book of Psalms*, 122.
6. Cole, *Midnight Experience*, 20.

(Psalm 32:1), concealed or 'forgiven' (Psalm 32:1) or lifted. Without this confession and type of walk, unhappiness and sorrow are themes, a drought in the soul is known (Psalm 32:4). However, when the Psalmist confessed in penitence, mercy was given:

> I acknowledge my sin unto thee, and mine iniquity have I not hid. I said, I will confess my transgressions unto the Lord; and thou forgavest the iniquity of my sin. Selah. (Psalm 32:5).

God appears for the psalmist like a hiding place, a refuge, and condescended to teach him. One cannot pray for guidance in good conscience without the conditions of verse 5 (cited above). The promise of verse 8 of Psalm 32 is contingent upon sincere confession: 'I will instruct thee and teach thee in the way which thou shalt go: I will guide thee with mine eye.' God's blessing cannot be assumed whilst living in unrepentant sin and clear direction will not be ascertained whilst living in rebellion to His will. You cannot realistically expect more light whilst not obeying the light He has given, a daily walking in the light with Him is required. However, Psalm 119 is not penned for our condemnation, rather written to the tune of magnifying God's grace towards His people in Jesus. [7]

The next verse in the Word of God, Psalm 119:5, has a lament coupled with an affirmation—that God commands, therefore he will obey His ways (or 'decrees' as the New International Version, NIV has). The lament is that he feels his feet take him where he would not always wish to go, and his eyes wander where is not healthy. Approaching the scriptures in obedience creates humility; the Psalmist grieves over the residual sin within and pleads that God would direct / govern his inclinations and actions towards Him. The successive verse continues the theme, that no shame would be felt when he looks at God's commands because his heart is already in a place where it can receive instruction and act accordingly. The Authorised Version (AV) of scripture notes: '. . . have respect unto all thy commandments.' (v.6) The Bible is not therefore a menu card to select things which are easier to keep. It is the psalmist's desire to implement all of God's Word.

7. Ash, *Bible Delight*, 13.

Verse 7 speaks of praise gushing from a heart which habitually desires what is right—'uprightness of heart'. Praise, mentioned 130 times in the AV version of psalms, is joy in God, His person and work—this expressed may be silent, quiet, with music or meditations upon Him. Whatever way it is practiced here, it is done so in a way which is right, a heart sprinkled with the blood of the scarified animal, pre-figuring what Christ would do by His atoning death on Calvary. The psalmist alludes to learning by sanctified experiences, the decisions of God, including as the Amplified scriptures note, the punishments for particular lines of impure and unholy deeds or thoughts. Against this backdrop of this thought the next verse (8) states he will keep his statues or decrees and pleads that God will not leave Him absolutely, entirely or completely. Feeling his own weakness, he recognises his incapacity to do what is right, he humbly cries and recognises the horror of falling into degrees of sin. He makes a plea for help rather than a resolution to do better, realising in himself he has a bias, a bent toward evil. The remaining sin and Adamic, fallen nature, as well as fleshly and worldly desires pull him back and grate upon him, he appeals to God in heaven for help.

9 BETH.

ט בַּמֶּה יְזַכֶּה-נַּעַר, אֶת-אָרְחוֹ—לִשְׁמֹר, כִּדְבָרֶךָ.	Wherewithal shall a young man cleanse his way? By taking heed thereto according to Thy word.

BETH, the second letter of this psalm, takes its meaning from the word 'house' and 'El' meaning 'God'. Moreover, Bethlehem is the 'house of bread' or 'Bethel', 'house of God.' God is like a house for those who know Him personally, to abide in Him in repentance and faith is essential. In addition, by maintaining fellowship in the house of God and applying God's Word, as the injunction is, the believer is kept on the right path (resisting sin and trusting wholly on Jesus). This scripture is most fitting for the younger and older brethren, both of which can be pulled by lust of various kinds, from sexual temptations to covetousness to worldliness. However, especially for young people, the world has prominent sexual advertising, freely available pornography and many nets to trap a person. The entertainment industry, a smokescreen for evil, booms with ungodly influences, driven by Satan, the orchestrator of this world's music, fashions and fads. Man's imagination of the heart is depraved from youth and unchecked it leads to an entire overcoming of one into the cesspit of iniquity. Worldlings may ensnare others, or seek them to conform to a mass homogeneity. David, in Psalm 140:5 evince the 'snare', 'cords', 'net' and gins' laid to destroy him. Equally, Psalm 69:1 asseverates the waters (of danger) almost drowning him. David couches doctrine and experiencing in graphic illustrative imagery—his reliance upon God.

Standing and staying on a path of purity is essential to holiness. The cleansing of one's way or path is through cleaning, purging and purifying; it is God Himself who does this by regeneration, His Word and the Spirit. The MacArthur Study Bible notes: 'Internalising the Word is a believer's best weapon to defend against encroaching sin.'[8] One way to begin to do this is to set no temptation or evil image before our eyes, no unclean thing which will feed lust and eventually spiral downwards. To fill the gap, where sin is removed from, a positive should be inserted, considering and meditating upon that which is lovely, pure, holy, right, just and so forth. This does not fuel lust but promotes godliness and holiness:

> Finally, brethren, whatsoever things are true, whatsoever things are honest, whatsoever things are just, whatsoever things are pure, whatsoever things are lovely, whatsoever things are of good report; if there be any virtue, and if there be any praise, think on these things. (Philippians 4:8).

The psalmist notes that with his whole heart he has sought the LORD; The Latin Vulgate of verse 10 states: *'in toto corde meo exquisivi te ne errare me facias a mandatis tuis'*. Due to this, he appears more assured (perhaps due to spiritual progress on the Christian journey?), than verse four, where he cries that his ways were directed to the law of God, here he asks that he may not stray, like a vagrant, from God and His commands. The image of sheep and

---

8. MacArthur, *McArthur Study Bible*, 851.

shepherd are inferred here; he sees himself desirous to obey but like a dumb lamb, easily led astray by the trappings of the world. The appeal to the heavenly shepherd of the soul is made, that He would vouchsafe his soul.

On a recent Birthday card, the sender inscribed verse 11 of Psalm 119, 'Thy word have I hid in my heart, that I might not sin against thee.' The English Standard Version (ESV) uses 'stored up' (based upon the nuanced term to hide or to treasure). Keeping the truth deep within the heart is essential to walking in holiness. Old Testament characters such as Daniel and Joseph are illustrative of those who kept the scriptures in their heart and mind and were kept despite diabolical temptations to sin. The placing of the truth within, like eating the word / scroll as Ezekiel did (Ezekiel 3:3) can be a difficult exercise, which takes time and effort. Yet, the laying up of God's Word is a precious thing, it helps protect us from our own thoughts and safeguards against sin. Bridges compares the worldly state to the spiritual state, when the Word written and incarnate dwelling by faith in the heart by the Spirit is loved:

> When the soul is thus conscious of 'following the Lord fully', there is a peculiar dread of wandering. In a careless or half-hearted state, wanderings are not watched, so long as they do not lead to any open declension. Secret prayer will be hurried over, worldly thoughts unresisted, waste of time in frivolous pursuits indulged, without much concern. Not so, when the heart is fully in pursuit of its object. There is a carefulness, lest wandering thoughts should become habitual. There is a resistance of the first step, that might lead into a devious path. The soul remembers the 'wormwood and the gall' (Lam. iii. 19), 'the roaring lion', and the devouring wolf; and in the recollection of the misery of its former wandering, dreads any departure from the Shepherd's fold.[9]

The contrast between walking in the light of God's Word and walking in darkness are seen in attitude and behaviour. Moreover, hurried devotions and a predisposition to wilfully sin are indicative of the poor spiritual state. However, when in obedience with God

9. Bridges, *Exposition of Psalm 119*, 21.

through His Word, what a difference-sin is resisted, the devil's roar more easily noticed and godly behaviour is exhibited.

The next verse continues a theme of praise, blessing God and asking Him to teach him His ways. The author asks God, the Divine author, to be his teacher and to guide him into truth, with the open scriptures before him. The term 'blessed' in verse 12 is a different Hebrew word than verses 1 and 2; it means to eulogise, praise or be illustrious מְהֻלָּל, it indicates that when we seek to hide God's Word in our inner man, we desire His statutes—they become our delight and we are not desirous for self-will. This promotes a prayerful and praising spirit within us, which should be a joy to do as, performed in the spirit of holiness, is a blessing to God and us; 'May my meditation be pleasing to Him, for I rejoice in the LORD' (Psalm 104:34).

The mouth and lips are to be used to praise God. The psalm in verse 13 states that his lips have declared, recounted or pronounced all the judgments, ordinances or decisions of God's will or Word. The believer, filled with the love of God and His Word, wants others to know all about the one He loves. Just as a mother loves her children with an intense depth of love, so it is in some small way we can understand God's love towards us. If operating within a functioning family, she desires others to know about how wonderful (even if he is not) her son is, as that is her rejoicing. When stirred to think upon God and what He has done for us and given us such a word, our lips move in praise as our hearts lift Him up, so we share in the proclamation of the gospel of grace. People recognised that 'never did a man speak like this'—no one had words or conduct like Christ (John 7:46). Verse 2 of Mary Artemesia Lathbury's hymn 'Break thou the bread of life' notes:

> Thou art the Bread of Life,
> O Lord, to me,
> Thy holy Word the truth
> That saveth me;
> Give me to eat and live
> With Thee above;
> Teach me to love Thy truth,
> For Thou art Love.[10]

10. Lathbury, *Break thou the bread of life*, verse 2.

No treasure can be compared to rejoicing in the richness of God's treasure store in His unchanging book. Verse 14 recognises that the way of God is better than any riches in this world, in fact, it notes the phrase—'all riches'. The merchant man, seeking goodly pearls, when he found the pearl of great price was not interested in any other treasure, he had what was worth more than anything in the world-Christ (Matthew 13:45-46). The importance of the spiritual discipline of meditating upon the scriptures is stressed in verse 15, as the author writes of fixing his eyes and respecting the testimonies of his God. The Hebrew term denotes pondering, musing and giving devotional time to thoughts, scanning a route (well-trodden path) of the LORD. Biblical meditation is 'in thy' (verses 15 and 23) word. There are examples and injunctions to apply oneself to study and scriptural (not Eastern, mythical) mediation—reflecting upon a text and prayerfully going through its implications. For instance, Isaac, in Genesis 24:63 meditated in the field in the evening—literally, it may be rendered—he 'talked with himself'. Joshua 1:8 reminds the people to meditate upon the law continually. Equally, Psalm 1:2 identifies that the behaviour of the believer will be one of perpetual scriptural mediation. The renewed mind, as Romans 12:1-2, is one absorbed in and controlled by God's word. 'Meditation is the *chewing* upon the truths we have heard . . . If it be inquired what meditation is, I answer—Meditation is the soul's retiring of itself, that by a serious and solemn thinking upon God, the heart may be raised up to heavenly affections.'[11]

Meditating upon passages of the Bible is not a spiritual trace state, it is disciplined thinking and reflecting deeply upon doctrine and God's works, this prevents wandering thoughts, vain ideas or sinful habits. Instead, it helps train and expand the mind to ponder the gems of His Word. This links to self-examination-rooting out sin, reflecting upon the awfulness of sin and what it has done and what allowing sin into your life will do. Meditation upon salvation helps promote gratitude for such a wonderful redemption, reflecting upon Christ and His beauty or the names of God foster love for Him. Finally, reflecting upon the eternality of life beyond the

---

11. Watson, *"Christian on the Mount,"* paras. 5, 6.

temporal affairs of this world, will likely stir our heart and transform conversation from sports, news or weather—to God. The frequent reflection upon scripture helps in walking aright and aids decision-making as the Word is already flowing through them. Job could say that he had not retreated from God's Word and that it was to him more vital than his necessary daily sustenance (Job 23:12).

Finally, in this stanza, the psalmist states that he will delight or solace in the decrees of His Lord and God, not forgetting them or being neglectful of the Word so that it becomes obscured or lost. Jesus spoke on several occasions about what we listen to and how we listen to it; taking heed to what we hear (Mark 4:24) and how we hear it, referent to the Word of life, (Luke 8:18). With this in mind, the believer's delight is to be in the edicts of God—they are to be immersed with godly influence and good company, who speak in edifying ways and encourage a good hearing of the Word. They are they which listen and seek to do as they hear (James 1:22). Thomas Manton succinctly summarises: 'The doers of the Word are the best hearers.'[12]

| גְּמֹל עַל-עַבְדְּךָ אֶחְיֶה; וְאֶשְׁמְרָה דְבָרֶךָ. יז | 17 GIMEL. Deal bountifully with Thy servant that I may live, and keep Thy word. |

GIMEL has the pictorial image of a foot running towards God's lovingkindness. This section therefore begins at verse 17 and concluding at verse 24, deals with holiness from the perspective petitioning God that He might 'deal bountifully' (v.17) with him so that he would obey His will. The term 'deal' in Hebrew is *'gamal'*, which means confer benefit upon. It is a striking thing to note that the psalmist identifies himself as a servant, similar to the Apostle Paul (Romans 1:1, as a 'bond servant') of God. Thus, the servant of God must surrender his own desires to do what He wants and not the inclination of his own fallen heart, which is untrustworthy and evil (Jeremiah 17:9). He prays for life to be lived and spent for God. I remember a sermon a number of years ago when an American evangelist and minister, preached on: 'I will most gladly spend

12. Manton, *Psalm 119: One Hundred and Ninety Sermons by Thomas Manton*, 132.

and be spent for your souls' (2 Corinthians 12:15). In so doing, he held up a bank note and reminded the congregation of being good spenders in God's kingdom, for the service of the master. The rationale was that at the Bema judgment (of 1 Corinthians 3) that Christians be rewarded by being servant hearted, using the gifts God has given them to the best of their ability and time they have. The second part of verse 17, deal 'bountifully' with me, refers to dealing fully, adequately, or, to wean or ripen. This cry is one of asking God to bless him with maturity in the faith by weaning him away from this world and ripening the fruits of the Spirit in his life.

As both verses 16 and 17 have highlighted, the author desires to learn and keep the Word of God. Now, the psalmist moves in verse 18 to wishing to gain spiritual insights into the depths of the Word. He prays 'open' my eyes—'galah'—this speaks of unveiling or uncovering any hindrance, that he might know 'wondrous things out of thy law.' The prayer request is that he might be bathed in the Word / saturate the reading of the Bible in prayer. Clearly, the verse notes the desire to dig deeper into the Word, seeing greater and clearer insights into each portion of the Word. He is not content with a surface reading of the Word or the superficial meaning but longs to know more. This has applicability for every Christian, that we look to the LORD for enhanced clarity on less clear verses and ask for a deeper knowledge of those scriptures which are easier to comprehend or more familiar ones. How we need to pray that God would take the scales of spiritual blindness from our eyes and enliven us with His Holy Spirit that we are quickened to life. In so doing, the psalmist asks God to manifest wonderful doctrines, miracles, the works of God and the hope we can have in Christ and most importantly—the person of Jesus.

Verse 19 acknowledges the Christian pilgrimage, a life of journeying in this world as a temporary resident to eternal life with the LORD. Peter acknowledges this fact and describes believers as 'strangers scattered' (1 Peter 1:1). These are they which are dispersed, who live by a different code to the world around them—the Word of God. To stand under the banner of the cross is to be at enmity with the world. It is likely that the recipients of the circular letter for Asia Minor (in modern Turkey) with regions and districts were seen as outcasts, aliens, belonging elsewhere. Verse 19 of the Psalm 119 takes up the theme—'I am a stranger in the earth.' Thus, he is a sojourner in the world, surrounded by people of this world who have their portion in this life (Psalm 17:14)—but by distinctive contrast, he is a citizen of God's kingdom. As such he has different desires to those around him, he wants the LORD and His ways. Holiness, is therefore, standing as a pilgrim in a world which is anti-God, swimming against the tides and currents of the flow of ungodly influences which come like a deluge against the LORD's people. Therefore, he prays that God would not hide His Word from him, this is his road map to the eternal glory.

The soul of the psalmist breaks, is overtaken by longing or is perpetually consumed by God's ordinances, judgments, decisions or justifications (verse, v.20). The term 'break' embedded within the verse expresses grief in the soul of overpowering emotion. The notion of being worn out or experiencing languish of the soul for fervent desire for the Word of life. In the Christian life the world can encroach significantly and drain the believer of life and vitality, individuals can be proud in their opposition to God. In the West, at present, the rise and rapid advances of secular humanism has left some believers known to the writer of this work as wearied. However, what are these plots to the LORD? But folly, just laughable (Psalm 2). The proud are said to be 'rebuked' (v.21), which disobey the scriptures and err wilfully ('*shagah*'). God hates pride (Proverbs 16:5) and resists those who present themselves in such a way (1 Peter 5:5,6; James 4:6). God will meet judgment upon those who are arrogant and oppose the truth. For example, Pharaoh, whose proud heart was hardened, despite God's warnings chose to disobey until there was no remedy, remaining wilful and a reprobate (see Exodus 8 and 9). By contrast, God loves those who are humble, respond with brokenness over sin and come with a teachable spirit to His Word. The child of God should subjugate pride and be clothed with humility, like the Lord Jesus Christ, who left heaven to be born in a shed, gazed upon by cattle He had created. Philippians reminds us that Christ's mind should be ours (Philippians 2:5-9); those who are saved and live in humility are they which have greater insights into the scriptures of truth.

A plea for the removal of 'reproach' (scorn) and 'contempt' (disdain) is now made (v.22). Feelings of scoffing, ridicule and disparagement are made against the author of the Psalm. The Hebrew 'contempt' has a nuanced meaning, referring to feelings of hatred as a result of their judgment against him, on account of prosperity or springing from evil. The term 'reproach' is an indicator that the psalmist is made to feel shame and disgrace for his ideas (having a personal relationship with God) or behaviour which is counter-cultural, the fruit of this relationship. In the advances we make toward heaven, there are forms of persecution from separations between believers and unbelievers, which can be emotionally distressing. Some endure psychological persecution—being made to feel foolish or even insane for following the Bible and believing in God. Others, often in other countries, recorded by organisations such as Barnabas, Open Doors, Release International and so forth help our brethren in places where God's people go through so much. The verse states that he 'kept' (v.22) God's ways, which is likely the ground on which his enemies are persecuting him. However, come what may, this is the essential duty of the believer, keeping true to God's Word even in a dark day. The awfulness of the experiences intensifies as the next verse, 23, notes how those in authority whispered lies and spoke treacherously against him. Rulers, chiefs, captains, officials and princes are at the root of those who assembled to speak slanderous lies against the psalmist. This would have been especially heart breaking as those in power are abusing their position to fight, unjustly against the author of the psalm. These dangerous opponents have power to seek to discredit, destroy, burn or take the scriptures out of circulation. However, God will vindicate—'Let God arise, let his enemies be scattered' (Psalm 68:1). God haters are ephemeral.

Finally, in this section, we come to verse 24: the testimonies are said to be his 'delight' שַׁעֲשֻׁעָי (ša·ă·šu·ʿāy) and 'counsellors' אַנְשֵׁי (ʾan·šê). There is a beauty in the psalmist's words that he is excited, awed, thrilled and gratified deeply by the Word of God. Chapman beautifully summarises: 'Man-made rules are burdensome and tedious, but God's testimonies should be a delight for the Christian.'[13]

---

13. Chapman, *Thy Word*, 30.

Second, the notion of being counselled by the book: Biblical counselling is most effective when the Bible is opened and there is prayer and the Holy Spirit ministers to a believer. The counsel from the scriptures teaches him how he should act, which is far superior to the wisdom of the world.

דָּבְקָה לֶעָפָר נַפְשִׁי; חַיֵּנִי, כִּדְבָרֶךָ .כה	25 DALETH. My soul cleaveth unto the dust; quicken Thou me according to Thy word.

DALETH takes it meaning from the word 'door'. The psalmist is weak and needy, yet the door is open to him as he seeks God. Jesus said, 'I am the door' of salvation or 'gate' in the NIV (John 10:9). This section (verses 25–32) begins with a solemn reminder of the battle believers are in; the things of the world are seeking to constantly draw us back away from God. The soul, in verse 25, is said to cling, lay low or cleave to 'the dust'. This recalls what happened to Adam, our ancestor. The ground was cursed after sin entered into the world by the federal head—Adam—and the consequences thereby meant thorns and toil would now be prevalent. This verse notes how the soul tries to go back to the world and continues to desire dusty attractions instead of the God of the Word. Therefore, he prays for reviving in the soul and for help then understanding even when suffering, he has soul sickness and likely lies prostrate, crying. However, Jay Adams writes how the scriptures, especially this psalm gives full guidance, and accompanied by the Spirit's work, is fully able to equip in all matters.[14] The Bible is good medicine for the soul, the Holy Spirit prescribes what is needed for us. Exposing oneself to the scriptures, taken with faith, helps to deal with the root sin and address his need (as it deals with people and principles). When in a low condition, he finds comfort and answers in the scriptures, taking one day at a time, avoiding anxiety (see Matthew 6:25).

The details for the psalmist's life are in the scriptures, he appears to have such confidence in the power of the Word, noting he will speak of His ways but states how he continues to need direction

14. Adams, *Counsel from Psalm 119*, 14.

and asks to be taught God's way (rather than relying upon his own ideas). Philip asked the Ethiopian Eunuch in Acts 8:30 if he understood what he was reading. He needed Philip, used by the Spirit of God, to open the scriptures of Isaiah to him to show the Messianic principles, and lead him to the knowledge of salvation through Jesus Christ, the one illustrated in the prophesy. Sometimes we can read without specific understanding of what God is saying and wanting to minister to us; in verse 27 the psalmist underlines the need of knowledge, 'Make me to understand the way of thy precepts'. The God of providence sometimes acts mysteriously—He is His own interpreter—He may shroud some aspects of His dealings with mankind and disclose other facets. This is His own prerogative but nonetheless the psalmist prays for clarity upon God's guiding rules. The well-known scripture is indicative of this matter.

> The secret things belong unto the Lord our God: but those things which are revealed belong unto us and to our children for ever, that we may do all the words of this law. (Deuteronomy 29:29).

The purpose of the Psalmist wishing to know God's law was not for intellect alone but to pass on the revelation to others. God commanded that the truth should be passed on to other generations (Deuteronomy 6:7; Psalm 78:4). Equally, the great commission, at the end of Matthew, chapter 28 and Mark, chapter 16, illustrate the significance of sending the truth to all who will hear. Thus, the Psalmist asks for understanding for divine duties—setting forth the great news—there would be a Messiah, who has now come, to save His people from their iniquities.

Next, 'My soul melteth for heaviness: strengthen thou me according to thy Word' (or *dabar*) (v.28). The soul is said to melt ('*dalaph*') for 'heaviness' ('*tugah*'). The Hebraic term for melting is used elsewhere in Ecclesiastes 10:18 as a descriptor of dilapidation on account of neglect. When in sin, David in Psalm 32 also stated how God's chastening caused loss of vitality and joy. This appears to be the case here as the next verse contextualises that it is his sin in view, he has been prone to falsehood and asks God to remove lying from his heart and lips. The writer states he wishes to turn away from 'lying', hypocrisy, formalism and be established by God, asking that God would privilege him with instruction. It is imperative that our hearts are engaged wholly in prayers and worship to God. We should be quick to repent, when this is not the case. The order here is significant, that repentance must come before instruction can be legitimately asked for and granted.

In verse 30, the writer has selected the right path; he has sought the way of righteousness: 'I have chosen the way of truth . . .' This indicates a resolute determination to select the path of truthfulness. A key question here is: do we have such a desire to follow after the right way or are we busy doing our own thing? The word 'righteousness' may also be translated 'faithfulness'. The verse continues in the affirmation that he has set the rules of God consciously before him. This if further expressed in verse 31 as he uses the term 'stuck' to express how he kept to God's mishpat and heeded it in practice. The Hebrew verb for cling or 'stuck' דָּבַק (dabaq) is the same word as used in verse 25 for 'cleave', meaning to join, cling, pursue or adhere. The mark of being faithful in the Christian life, a key feature of holiness, is to stick close to God's truth, which makes one grow and develop spiritual vitality.

The close of Daleth (verse 32) is the prayer that God would give such spiritual energy in granting breadth of understanding in the heart or mind to run the way of the *mitsvah* (commandments). The term 'enlarge my heart' can be rendered 'make my heart broad' ('*rachab*'); the expanded ability to perceive the truth. Moreover, Isaiah 60:5 notes how the heart will fear and be enlarged. It is the duty but great joy of the believer to have expanded views (based upon the scriptures) of God. This is implemented when we earnestly seek for such experiences upon our knees with humble dependency that God would show us more of Himself. As a consequence, we have a clearer understanding of His will for us and we grow in the grace of Him and 'run the way of His commands', as an athlete would compete in a race with zeal and exertion to win the prize. Paul wrote of fighting 'the good fight of faith' (1 Timothy 6:12) and running the race of life before us, dispensing with sin and all its encumbrances (Hebrews 12:1).

33 HE. Teach me, O LORD, the way of Thy statutes; and I will keep it unto the end.	לג. הוֹרֵנִי יְהוָה, דֶּרֶךְ חֻקֶּיךָ; וְאֶצְּרֶנָּה עֵקֶב.

The undergirding in this section is prayer for instruction or command as directed by the term 'HE': 'Teach me' (v.33), 'Give me' (v.34), 'Make me' (v.35), 'Incline me' (v.36), 'Turn me' (v.37). 'Stablish me' (v.38) and 'Turn me' (v.39). The opening of the stanza begins with the request of the Holy Spirit to grasp our way and comprehend our responsibility to the perceptive will of God—Yahweh would make the statutes (*choq*) plain before him. The Spirit is needed to illuminate truths to us and apply them to our hearts, consciences and souls. Solomon is a clear example of one who sought God for His heart—an '. . .understanding heart. . .' (1 Kings 3:9), literally 'a hearing heart'. Verse 34 highlights, with synonymous parallelism, the desire for 'understanding' of the law of God (Torah) with a clear view to keep it not in part or the sections which are more appealing but the entirety of it with his 'whole heart'. The importance of going in God's way is stressed as he asks God to 'make' him to go in the pathway of obedience—the true character of a regenerate person. The commandments (*mitsvah*) of God is where his delight is found, true joy is found doing His will, living sacrificially and lovingly; Jesus spoke and reminded us that: 'If you know these things, happy are ye if you do them' (John 13:17).

The theme continues in verse 36, he asks to be awakened to the love letter to his soul—the Word of the LORD. He asks: 'Incline my heart unto thy testimonies' (*eduth*)—the inclining means stretch out, draw forth or predispose, focusing the thoughts, affections and therefore, daily choices towards God. David specifically asks God to direct his heart towards His ways. Unless we conscientiously ask God for this, we will be covetous in our desires and the overflow of this, in our behaviour. He asks that his inclination would be for God's ways and 'not covetousness' (the greed for more), whether materially or in taking excessive leisure time or for recognition of higher status in the world. Indeed, Jesus warned, in the parable of the rich man who grew great crops and engaged in a selfish building project of significant expansion, that he would have nothing to show for eternity when his soul was called for account. We are to, 'Take heed, and beware of covetousness: for a man's life consisteth not in the abundance of the things which he possesseth' (Luke 12:15).

Next, the clause in verse 37 asks God to 'turn' the Psalmist's eyes away from another sin, that of vanity, deceit or emptiness. The Hebrew verb turn can be translated 'to pass over' or 'through'. The implication, that God would allow our eyes to pass over things which are of no spiritual benefit (especially those things which are iniquitous). Sometimes our behaviour is shaped by pursuing worthless things, which take away our attention from eternal matters and do not help us meet the injunction of minding heavenly things (Colossians 3:1). The thing which occupies our thoughts and time is likely to be that which controls us and shapes our behaviour. The question is to be asked: what do we think and talk about most of the time? This could be our idol (if not Christ), which is best plucked from our hearts. The Psalmist asks that his eyes may be moved towards higher priorities and not consumed by the temporal.

The final verses in this section deal with the 'quickening' which is needful to combat sin and walk in the newness of the life which the Spirit brings. Being awakened to the LORD's ways means that we do not follow dead religion, formality or emptiness. Thus, the writer expresses that his longing and time would be for God's Word, that which is of the greatest value. 'Stablish thy word unto thy servant' (v.38), is a plea which shows how he wishes to raise up in his estimation God's Word, recognising his servitude to it. This approach is evidenced in the sentiments 'who is devoted to thy fear', the reverence of God is a blessing to the soul and seen as a sign of great wisdom (a reoccurring theme of Proverbs, such as in Proverbs 9:10). Such reverence aims for loving obedience to the best of masters.[15]

As well as turning his eyes away from vain things, the Psalmist asks that God would 'turn away my reproach' (v.39) or disgrace / contumely which is from the root meaning, of the pudenda. Some scorn comes from the ungodly, however, the greatest feeling of disgrace is when we know we have sinned against love (as God's ways

15. De Moss, Holiness. The Heart God Purifies, 13.

are acknowledged as 'good', verse 39). Sin deadens our consciences and makes us feel disgraceful to a holy God; Psalms 32 and 51 clearly illustrate this point, as David cries out in feelings of anguish and sorrow as God is grieved with him—and this is clearly felt in the soul. Finally, HE concludes in verse 40 with the reminder that despite propensity to sin, he longs for the precepts of God. Peter is an illustrative example of this, whose love for Jesus was imperfect, even to the point of denial. Yet, he was forgiven, restored and re-commissioned in the service of God.

מא וִיבֹאֻנִי חֲסָדֶךָ יְהוָה; תְּשׁוּעָתְךָ, כְּאִמְרָתֶךָ.	41 VAU. Let Thy mercies also come unto me, O LORD, even Thy salvation, according to Thy word.

VAU, the sixth letter of Psalm 119, has the attached symbol of a nail or hook. The connecting hook, used in Exodus 27:9-10, were silver hooks to hold the curtain (*yeriah*) to enclose the tabernacle in which God's holiness dwelt. Each verse of this stanza begins with a conjunctive; beginning with the iterative theme of the imparta- tion of holiness through receipt of the new birth by God's mercy, or unmerited favour. To underscore this, he writes of the undeserving and covenant loyalty God has towards His people; he pleads that salvation will come through the Word of God—that is specifically all His promises. He then turns his attention to having an answer to those who reproach him (v.42). In the days of Noah there were many scoffers. As in Lot's day, God's servants can often feel mar- ginalised by opposition but are to depend wholeheartedly upon the God of the Book. God, sometimes in His grace, saves even the worst indifferent or scornful individuals. The Psalmist's confidence is aligned with the Word of life and knows that this word spoken in the power of the Spirit can deal with the reproaches of his oppo- nents. The word of God is likened to a hammer breaking the rocky or stony heart (Jeremiah 23:29). The scriptures within the heart and mouth help one to have a firm confidence in the instrumentality of the LORD's service. If nothing spiritual is within the heart, how will there be godly things proceeding forth from one's lips? This is the prayer of the Psalmist (v.43), that truth might be within the heart and mouth, so that others might be influenced for good by it.

The longevity of obedience is expressed in the remarks that he will seek to obey the law (Torah) in steadfast constancy, 'So shall I keep thy law continually forever and ever' (v.44). Blessings follow such a path of love for God—'liberty' is granted in obeying the precepts (*piqqud*) (verse 45). The term 'liberty' means 'in a wide place.' Today, true freedom from the cruel jailor of sin and Satan is in view—but when released, spiritual freedom is found in Jesus: 'whom the Son sets free is free indeed' (John 8:36). If one has been saved and no longer in the grip of Satan, they will have opportunities to testify of this, even before those in high positions in the world. Verse 46 records the opportunities of testimony before kings, this is echoed in Matthew 10:18 and Luke 21:34. Philippians 1:12–14 records how the whole of the palace guard heard the gospel—the Apostle Paul had frequent occasions where he spoke to leaders including Felix, Festus, Agrippa and Nero. On one occasion, under the power of the Holy Ghost, Felix trembles with conviction (see Acts 24).

Finally, this section concludes with the expression of delight towards God's commandments, which he affirms he loves (v.47). This has been the key to the entire psalm—love of God and His truth—which he wants to obey. Perhaps it could be said to be a clear summary of Biblical holiness? This is re-iterated as his hands are lifted up to fulfil God's commands, which he loves and meditates upon. The writer is asking God, to whom his hands are raised for divine help to do His commands, as this is the way he desires to take. At the culmination of this psalm, David appears lost for words, caught in wonder, love and praise-awed by God. The expression of lifted hands (verse 48) towards the *mitsvah* and love of the *choq* is an expression of the heart being in subjected surrender to obedience of God and His ways. Akin asks: 'What does it mean to think more about God than yourself?'[16]

16. Akin, *Exalting Jesus in Psalms 119*, 111.

מט זְכֹר־דָּבָר, לְעַבְדֶּךָ—עַל, אֲשֶׁר יִחַלְתָּנִי.	49 ZAIN. Remember the word unto Thy servant, upon which thou hast caused me to hope.

ZAIN 'sword' or 'weapon' with a derived root inferring sustenance or nourishment. The Sword of God, His word, is the source
of food that the hungry soul needs to feed on by faith. The means
of grace (the scriptures) incorporated within prayer and praise;
the Psalmist seeks fulfilment in the Word for which his hope is
built. Hope, according to Hebrews 11:1, is the 'substance of things
hoped for the evidence of things not seen.' The 'substance' is the
same Greek word used elsewhere for 'confidence' (Hebrews 3:14).
Confident trust in the scriptures grants the child of God the essence
of what God promises those who know and love Him. The word
'evidence' is a legal term—'demonstration', referring to an assurance
of what has been guaranteed. Therefore, faith is not wishful thinking, it is a guarantee of eternal life in heaven with Him. Paul writing
to the church at Colossae, explains how a mystery known only by
the revelation of God has occurred and therefore, God's display of
salvation meant that those who have trusted in Jesus as the Messiah
were saved and had the assurance of: 'Christ in you, the hope of
glory' (Colossians 1:27).

In trials, the Psalmist uses personal pronouns, 'my' and 'me', he
states, that the Word of God provides comfort (Psalm 119:50). The
word (imrah) also brings him to life and helps him see with spiritual discernment, offering a word in season to overcome weariness
through the erosion of oppression upon the soul. The solace from
the Bible, applied to our circumstances, means that when distressed
the verses of scripture can minister to us. This helps with understanding God's providence in the trial and how one may be helped
come through the other end without damage to their faith (in fact,
actually strengthening it). There exists divine wisdom mingled with
love in every trial and cross; 1 Peter 1:7 states: 'That the trial of your
faith, being much more precious than of gold that perisheth'.

Insolent, presumptuous individuals have held the Psalmist in
'derision', הֱלִיצֻנִי (hĕ·lî·ṣu·nî) (v.51), they arrogantly mock and taunt
him. Yet, in all of this, the writer states that he has not swayed from

obeying the Torah. This provides a powerful lesson to Christians; the words and actions of men should simply drive us to prayer and an unshakeable vow to stand upon the Bible. This is echoed in verse 52, as the author notes how remembering God's past dealings with him 'of old' fortifies confidence for the future. The God of great promises cannot lie, repent and is immutable, His judgments (*mishpat*) are irrevocable and inerrant.

A striking word in verse 53 is noted: 'horror' takes hold of him as he sees the 'wicked that forsake thy law'. The term זַלְעָפָה 'zalaphah', 'horror' is only used on two other occasions in the scriptures (Psalm 11:6 and Lamentations 5:10), as it is a strong phrase meaning 'raging heat' or 'burning indignation.' This identifies such feeling that God's law has been violated, that he bubbles with righteous anger (like our Lord in the temple of money changers, see Matthew 21:12, 13; Mark 11:15–18). He sees infidels living in reckless regard for God's rules and is grieved and angered. It is most sad when we become spiritually amnestied to the downgrade of society and its attitudes towards the Bible and things of true religion. An alternative way of understanding 'horror' is the trembling sorrow the Psalmist feels when he sees the word ignored. In so doing, God Himself is spurned and the people fall under God's judgment.

In second part of verse 53—'the wicked that forsake thy law', the Hebrew 'forsake' denotes 'loosed', as if to cast it off. Christians should be moved when seeing the state of a nation falling into the darkness of night. Such a condition leads to admittance into the eternal hell. Physically, the place has charred, blackened walls. Psychologically, painful regret permeates the place. It is sad when the church for the large part, seems indifferent to this. This was not so for the Psalmist; he loved God and loved the things He loved and hated the things He hated. By contrast to the wicked, the writer states that God's laws and dealings with man is what causes him to sing. A merry, praising heart comes from the overflow of God's love and consideration of God's goodness to them. Praise assists the pilgrim on their way to heaven whilst in a temporal body, with an eternal soul, as a sojourner. Christians are temporal, alien residents, who belong elsewhere, passing through this world, looking towards the eternal heavens. Their outlook is upwards with a heavenly perspective. Such are not wedded to the passing things of this world and so absorb some hardships and pray for those who reject the scriptures and them (as followers of Jesus Christ).

As this section of the Psalm (119) draws to an end, the final two verses, 55 and 56, state how in the day and night he is remembering his God. *Piqqud* or precepts are God's detailed instructions, David states he knows the way he should go because of his adherence to the Torah. However, especially at night, the enemy can attack the Christian, as they can be tired and vulnerable. The power of many men's battles can be strong. However, the Psalmist here reminds us of a way of help: 'to remember thy name', calling upon God in the night seasons and from your bed. This undoubtedly helps begin the next day in a way which glorifies God as it is virtually impossible to sin at the same time as when remembering to pray. The study of God's name is remarkable, the various names of God something of His divine attributes. Equally, how He has chosen to reveal Himself to us and how He has worked in the lives of His servants of old is a profitable study. Paul writes to Timothy: 'Study to shew thyself approved unto God, a workman that needeth not to be ashamed, rightly dividing the word of truth' (2 Timothy 2:15).[17]

נז חֶלְקִי יְהוָה אָמַרְתִּי—לִשְׁמֹר דְּבָרֶיךָ.	57 CHETH. Thou art my portion, O LORD: I have said that I would keep Thy words.

CHETH (or Khet, Kheth, Chet, Het, or Heth) is about regeneration, resurrection and new life. The number of grace (*chen*) is eight, thus this eighth section of Psalm 119 commences with acknowledgement that God is his LORD on account of His salvation and mercy. The verse, 57, could equally be rendered, this is my portion, O LORD, to keep your word. There are two cross-references which identify the 'portion', Psalm 16:5, where God is the portion of his inheritance and Psalm 73:26, that God is his eternal portion even when this body decays, God will receive him. As a result, he is resolved to treasure and keep the Word of life.

17. Gowens, *A study of God's Hebrew Names*.

The next verse (58) is the entreaty of the Psalmist to the God of the scriptures (*imrah*) to be favourable to him and be a recipient of His mercy. His appeal is to the author of the Word of God to remember His Word and show mercy (favour, '*panim*' to whom none should necessarily be given). The writer was undoubtably familiar with God's acts as recorded in the formation of scriptures at that time and also experientially in the things he had learnt about from his own life experiences. With a sincere heart, favour is prayed for. As the Psalmist thinks upon God's ways, so his feet take the path of obedience to His eduth 'testimonies' (v.59). The term 'thought' comes from the Hebrew verb 'to weave'. The believer considers their own conduct and seeks to bring this into conformity with God's truth, consciously choosing God's way and forfeiting self-interest. The notion of self-examination (as linked to meditation) is concerned with 'thought on my ways' from the verb to plait or weave,[18] giving specific attention to detail. Think about what our life looks like before a holy God and how brief and fragile life is, like a web, which is easily destroyed. These things have a sanctifying effect, in seeking to walk far from the defects (manner, disposition or demeanour). In so doing, there is no procrastination, he states that: 'I made haste, and delayed not to keep thy commandments' (v.60). The verb חוש 'haste' (*chuwsh*) means responding with eagerness or excitement towards the *mitsvah*, commands—His Divine judgments and actions. The swiftness to be an obedient believer in word and deed is the essential ingredient in holiness. The backslider will be cold, insensitive to the work of the Holy Spirit and filled with self. Proverbs 14:14 notes: 'the backslide in heart is filled with his own ways.' By contrast, the vibrant Christian will be filled with God's ways and want to do His bidding.

The 'bands of the wicked have robbed me' (v.61), the ropes or measuring lines are said to encompass him, but he remembers His God. Snares or cords are surrounding him. Unsurprisingly, he desires to be loosed. The binding of cords may be used to picture the criminalising of a person (Paul was beaten and bound for his gospel witness, 2 Timothy 2:9). Equally, the sacrificial typology of

---

18. DeYoung, *The Hole in Our Holiness*, 13.

Isaac in Genesis 22:9, pre-figuring the Lord Jesus, who was bound for sentence (Matthew 27:2) depicts binding as a means of judging. In Psalm 119:61, as the writer is bound by metaphorical attacks, judged and criminalised for his witness, he embraces and shares in a small measure of the suffering of Jesus. As Christians stand for Christ, society has sought to bind gospel witness by criminalising Biblical, moral and ethical teachings. As God speaks in tender tones during the time of pandemic, coronavirus may help some to re-calibrate their ideas towards the gospel. Those who still vehemently oppose God, He will deal with them in terrifying tones at the end of life (Psalm 9:16–17).

Despite being under spiritual attack, David has a mind to-wards God's righteousness. 'At midnight I will rise to give thanks unto thee because of thy righteous judgments' (Psalm 119:62). At this hour the Psalmist's soul could have been in the blackest spiritual state (so distressed, refusing to be comforted, Psalm 77:3). However, we read: 'At midnight I will rise to give thanks unto thee because of thy righteous judgments' (Psalm 119:62). Thanksgiving is a beautiful exercise as it reminds us of all that we have in God and all He has done for our soul. Tell out my soul, the Magnificat or praise over the incarnation (Luke 1:46–55), written by Timothy Dudley Smith highlights such a theme.[19]

Thankfulness benefits our relationship with God, meaning that we do not approach God for a list of needs but just take time to be thankful and praise his name.

In the penultimate verse, 63, it records the author as a 'com-panion', a friend, a brother, a united associate with others who fear God and keep his rules and ordinances. Brotherly love should be apparent in Christian circles; there is no excuse for coldness among the LORD's people. The phrase 'birds of a feather, stick together', believers should regularly meet with likeminded Christians to fel-lowship, evangelise and break bread as they worship God (Acts 2:46). Malachi writes of the behaviour of believers and how God hears, remembers and blesses:

19. Smith, *"Tell Out, My Soul,"* verse 1.

Then they that feared the LORD spake often one to another: and the LORD hearkened, and heard *it*, and a book of remembrance was written before him for them that feared the LORD, and that thought upon his name. (Malachi 3:16).

Finally, the stanza closes which a crescendo of praise, verse 64 says: 'The earth, O LORD, is full of thy mercy: teach me thy statutes.' The lovingkindness of God covers the entire land (nothing escapes such pity), evidenced in creation and all over His works. Thus, the only right, fitting response, from a regenerate heart, is praise: a re-occurring theme within the psalm and the entire tenor of scripture. It is as if the Psalmist cannot contain himself and wants to sound a great 'Hallelujah!'

סה טוֹב, עָשִׂיתָ עִם-עַבְדְּךָ—יְהוָה, כִּדְבָרֶךָ.	65 TETH. Thou hast dealt well with Thy servant, O LORD, according unto Thy word.

TETH, the ninth letter of the acrostic psalm, orientates God's absolute rectitude and ultimate goodness. Verses 65 to 72 deal with the theme of promoting holiness through refining the character in affliction / suffering. A mature reflection is contained in verse 65, that states that God has dealt prudently with him according to His own word / will and purpose (*dabar*). The Psalmist asks God to train him in good taste / discernment. The term 'teach', verse 66, comes from the Hebrew noun for 'rod', used to direct in the right way. Subsequently, the transliterated version of the Hebrew (for verse 65) notes the goodness of JEHOVAH in His dealings with the writer, in accordance to His Word. Job 11:6 reminds us that 'God exacteth of thee less than thine iniquity deserveth.' The term 'exacteth' is a word meaning to forget the loan or borrowing and allow part of the sin debt to be forgotten. Equally, the forgiveness of the King in the parable of the king and servant, Matthew 18:24–27, illustrates the enormity of debt owed, illustrative of our debt and guilt towards God yet the king mercifully acquits the servant, pardoning all the guilt / cancelling the debt. Unbelievers or young in the faith can sometimes make ill-advised comments in the face of opposition. However, God has done as His will is. The prayer for sound knowledge and discernment is made (v.66). David asks literally for 'taste', the Hebrew translation of 'judgment', referring to spiritual discernment. This finds a similarity in Solomon's request to God for wisdom to rule well and make righteous, clear decisions (1 Kings 3; 1 Chronicles 3). We need to pray such prayers as we are prone to wander into our own ways and to make foolish decisions based upon our own wills and lusts from the old man nature and sinful heart. This is not simply reforming their ways; it is a 'new self' transformation and appropriating decisions based upon this nature.[20]

In verse 67, David was 'afflicted', humbled or bowed down; 'Before I was afflicted I went astray but now have I kept thy word' (v.67). The affliction of the writer, recorded in verse 67, explains prior to illness, persecution, distress (whatever the nature of it was), that he was in a worse spiritual state. Thus, the affliction accomplished good for his soul. This is a hard thing to write as no believer relishes troubles, difficulties or pain but here the experience of the Psalmist is he is afflicted and now walks closer to His God. 'Now have I kept thy word', at the close of verse 67. It is his experience that the pain brought a better situation, he cleaved to the Word as he had not done so. He also re-affirms that the affliction was good as learning took place-God's school of learning (v.71). Sometimes when things run smoothly our devotions can be less meaningful than when in the fiery furnace. The affirmation that God is good (v.68) and does good driving him to the *imrah*. When working recently in a Church school, at the commencement of assembly, the headteacher used to liturgically open with: 'God is good', the reply of the children and staff was to be: 'all the time, God is good.' Perhaps we need to be reminded as these children were of the goodness of God perpetually? Our thinking is then aligned and sometime corrected to realising how good God is in whatever circumstance. Only God is good (Luke 18:19).

By contrast, the 'proud' stir up lies, sow seeds of discord and seek the damage or destruction of believers (v.69). David uses the term 'forged a lie', literally 'smeared me with a lie', fitting imagery of

---

20. Carson, *NIV Biblical Theology Study Bible*, 2145.

the description to the way grease may be applied to the frying pan or baking tin. A smear campaign (using negative propaganda) to damage the reputation of another is the discrediting tactics used by the unrighteous. The Psalmist claims first-hand experience of being lied about, people influenced by the devil ('father of lies', John 8:44) are used to speak evil against him. However, he notes that he will keep the ways of God fully. In verse 70, the image of grease is used to depict the heart of the ungodly. The grease of the heart is gross, insensitive, thick and not able to be penetrated—this is used as a descriptor of their unconverted, rebellious heart. Moreover, the NIV renders this verse, in relation to their wicked heart as, 'callous and unfeeling.' These terms indicate an unsympathetic outlook with a cruel disregard for the welfare of others.

Finally, despite the animosity of the proud in heart, the law of God (*Torah*) is so precious to him, that it is seen as of more value than much money. A significant number of shekels of great value cannot compare to the value of the word of the living God. What is temporal wealth without Christ? Knowing Christ, who to know is the sum and substance of true wisdom, makes one eternally rich (Proverbs 3:14). The following verse in the hymn 'I'd rather have Jesus' illustrates this point most beautifully:

> I'd rather have Jesus than silver or gold I'd rather be his than have riches untold. I'd rather have Jesus than houses or land.
>
> Yes, I'd rather be led by his nail pierced hands
>
> Than to be the king of a vast domain and be held in sins dread sway I'd rather have Jesus than anything this world affords today.[21]

עג יָדֶיךָ עָשׂוּנִי, וַיְכוֹנְנוּנִי; הֲבִינֵנִי, וְאֶלְמְדָה מִצְוֹתֶיךָ.	73 IOD. Thy hands have made me and fashioned me; give me understanding, that I may learn Thy commandments.

21. Beverly-Shea, *I'd rather have Jesus*, verse 1.

The tenth section of this great psalm acknowledges God to be the author and creator of all things (also see Psalm 139), this is humbling when compared to the puniness of man. In Genesis 2:7, God created man (*Adam*) from the ground (*adamah*), breathing life into his nostrils. Moreover, Isaiah 64:8 deploys the images clay and a potter. The clay symbolising man and the potter, God, who forms man with His hands, like a craftsman shaping a vessel.

This is an important starting point: that the LORD is acknowledged to have the power to do anything, creating life out of nothing, sustaining all things and acting in the affairs of men. The Psalmist humbly asks God for His counsel to live thereby and survive in an 'alien world'.[22] This recognises his need of enlightenment and asks for help to see as He would have him see not in some humanistic way but what is right in His sight. Next, he interweaves a valuable lesson, that we need Christian fellowship (v.74) to share our love of God with and learn more of Him (as discussed above).

The next verse, verse 75, states God's goodness in sovereignty over the affairs of men. Exodus 34:6, 7:

> And the LORD passed by before him, and proclaimed, The LORD, The LORD God, merciful and gracious, longsuffering, and abundant in goodness and truth, keeping mercy for thousands, forgiving iniquity and transgression and sin. . .

The writer affirms that God's ways are correct, His dispositions are transcendently holy and just, and thus, he has been afflicted righteously (not in an arbitrary manner). God's judgments are literally rendered as 'righteous.' The term for 'afflictions' means 'to chasten' or 'to humble.' God's verdicts are right; we see things through a limited lens but Jehovah sees what is fitting and beneficial for us. However, this does not mean that he does not feel the pain of the condition he is in and therefore, supplicates God for comfort in distress according to the *imrah* (v.76). The secret prayer life involving thanking God for His providences, even if the meaning is not yet apparent, and praying for help, is a vital key to unlocking why the Psalmist can be so blessed when in distress. Noting the relative

---

22. Kidner, *Psalms 73-150*, 458.

conjunction in verse 77—'for' כִּי (kî–) God's mercy from His law is the source of his supreme joy.

The proud make an appearance in the psalm and are mentioned again in verse 78 (as with verse 69). They are said to deal in perverseness, twisted, deceitfulness without specific reason for such behaviour. Equally, Jeremiah laments the twisting of a matter in the context of a lawsuit: 'To subvert a man in his cause, the Lord approveth not' (Lamentations 3:36). Jesus was hated without a cause (Psalm 69:4; John 15:25) and falsehoods were vehemently employed at His mock trials before the Sanhedrin, Pilate and Herod (see Matthew 26 ff; Mark 15 ff; Luke 22 ff). Consequently, the disciple should expect no less as they seek to follow in the footsteps of the one who trod such a path of insults, loneliness and rejection. As with verse 69, the Psalmist resorts to reading and reflecting upon the scriptures, it is here he takes refuge until the enemy retreats as God arises and appears for him.

Finally, within this section, the last two verses (79 and 80) put forth the importance of how the fear of God brings a turning and a cleaving to the LORD. As a result, the heart is made right when such a turning is made. There is a necessity in re-evaluating our confidence in Him because we can easily wander and then have the most unworthy thoughts of the Saviour. It is the plea of verse 80: 'Let my heart be sound in thy statutes; that I be not ashamed.' 'Statutes' are the boundaries, *choq* of God and His ways; 'sound' comes from the Hebrew root adjective 'blameless' or 'truthful', with integrity. The key to this verse is soundness in doctrine and rectitude in behaviour, as directed by the scriptures. The heart is opposed to God by our Adamic nature and therefore, the verse asks for truthful, complete and wholesome approaches to interpret the scriptures that 'shame' does not come upon him. This 'shame' (paleness, delay or disappointment) can come through various avenues such as unintentionally committing acts of omission or commission against God. We must therefore be on our guard that we do not shame the cause of Christ by what we do or fail to do for the LORD.

פא כָּלְתָה לִתְשׁוּעָתְךָ נַפְשִׁי; לִדְבָרְךָ יִחָלְתִּי.	81 CAPH. My soul fainteth for Thy salvation; I hope in thy word.

CAPH, the 11th Hebrew letter of the alphabet, comes from the term 'to contain' (as a goblet or basin / bowl might hold liquid). The scriptures of truth contain those things necessary for salvation and sanctification; the Psalmist opens this stanza with the soul panting, fainting, longing for God's deliverance. Verses 81 and 82 use the same Hebrew word for 'fainteth' and 'fail' (meaning to accomplish, cease or end). These verses are multi-layered: a looking for personal deliverance from the enemies which were clearly perplexing him. The second reference is that salvation may be known to others, they may be saved from their sins. Finally, the third implication being, the old testament dispensation, where the people looked forward to the promised Messiah. This was a cause of great blessing but longing for the One to come. Here, the writer in verse 81, has his eyes towards God praying He would work in these three ways: bring help, send the Anointed One and visit the nation in reviving work. It is with a depth of inner longing that he is desirous of these mercies. The Lord Jesus, in Luke 22:15, conveys deep intensity: 'With desire I have desired to eat this passover with you before I suffer.' This was that His death would bring about the salvation that the psalmist cried for.

Verses 82 and 83 are cries for personalised deliverance, that comfort may be felt again as David trusts in the Word (*imrah*) and statutes (*choq*). In verse 82, he asks, in distress: '. . . When wilt thou comfort me?' He likens his experience, in verse 83, to feeling dry and uses a picture of a bottle or wineskin in smoke, hanging on rafters, shrivelling by means of the smoke, drying up to stiffen the skin. This could explain a season of spiritual dryness and a sense of distance from God, when one has to fight for joy in the LORD and actively seek to desire after Him.[23] The writer may be experiencing persecution for the Word's sake (Mark 4:17). After explaining how he feels, David calls for judgment upon his enemies who have contributed to this feeling (v.84). Moreover, they are persecuting him and evidently creating significant distress. The absence of immediate judgment causes him to ask why they have not yet been judged. Proverbs 13:12 states that 'hope deferred makes the heart sick.'

23. Piper, *When I Don't Desire God*, 20.

However, it must be remembered that the judge of all the earth will do what is right and acts righteously (Genesis 18:25). The proud are cited in verse 85 who dig holes or pits for him to fall into, which are not in keeping with God's law; they have created concealed holes in a deliberate attempt for his downfall. Sometimes these pits are literal, or more obvious attacks. In Genesis 37:24, Joseph was thrown down a pit after his brothers resented his prophetic dreams. Equally, Jeremiah, in Jeremiah 38:6, experienced similar treatment when he spoke as God's mouthpiece to the people—he was cast into a cistern pit. Such behaviour, as verse 86, denotes, is unlawful and results out of 'proud' (v. 85) unyielding spirits who resent the call to repent and follow God and therefore misuse His servants. The blessing for the believer is they are rescued from all pits, just as Joseph and Jeremiah were, so God looks after His own. The Psalmist in Psalm 40:2 speaks of spiritual deliverance from a 'horrible pit.' Christians have been freed from the pit of sins and blessed with the applied blood of Christ's propitiation (*hilasterion*)—which removes all of the Father's wrath against them (Romans 3:25).

Believers must be careful that wicked opponents of the gospel do not entice them to sin or stumble spiritually. Although deliverance and restoration is available, better not to lose your testimony with the church and world by falling in the first place. The Psalmist recognises that pits have been hewn and notes they are 'pits for me'. Being aware of the plots and some of the devices of the enemy is helpful, this decreases the likelihood of being caught off guard or ambushed. Verse 86 affirms all of God's ordinances to be right but as he seeks to act upon them, so he is persecuted the more. All who desire to lead holy lives will suffer persecution (2 Timothy 3:12). This is because the witness is opposing the cultural norms and withstanding the evil of the day. Psalm 102:6-7, the prayer of the afflicted, notes: 'I am like a pelican of the wilderness: I am like an owl of the desert. I watch, and am as a sparrow alone on the housetop.' There are three birds mentioned, which are out of place, in the wrong environment. The pelican is a water bird of Uganda which breeds, the owl is of the forest and finally, the sparrow is a communal rather than solitary bird. These images concur with how Psalm 119 portrays the pilgrim experience: out of place in the world and all alone. This is why the Psalmist cries 'help thou me' (Psalm 119:86).

David's persecutors had almost overpowered him or 'consumed' him, from the term *kalah* 'spent' or 'finished'. The breakthrough comes in the last two verses of CAPH, the enemies had nearly overtaken the writer but what was it that held him? 'But I forsook not thy precepts' (v.87). He listened, obeyed and trusted God to vindicate him by His *piqquid*, he had not been side-tracked from doing God's will. Finally, verse 88 concludes with the plea to 'quicken me after thy lovingkindness', revive him and give him life. Spiritual refreshment is vital all the time in the Christian pilgrimage but especially after severe testing. Psalm 92 is a reminder of the need to be anointed with 'fresh oil' (v.10) to experience God with freshness, which returns vitality to our soul. This vitality is achieved as we co-operate with God's covenantal stipulations (*eduth*) and appreciate His 'lovingkindness', loyalty to His people. An aspect of a holy life is one cleansed, sanctified and renewed by the Holy Spirit giving us fresh insights of Him, His will and ways. As this section closes, the author concludes: 'I will keep the testimonies of thy mouth.' God's breathed-word (2 Timothy 3:16) is authoritative in all matters and to be willingly adhered to.

פט לְעוֹלָם יְהוָה—דְּבָרְךָ, נִצָּב בַּשָּׁמָיִם.	89 LAMED. Forever, O LORD, Thy word is settled in heaven.

Verse 89 states the Word is 'settled', or 'stationed' in the dwelling place of God. The firmly set or placed word abides in heaven with God who is immutable. God is the author of the scriptures and establishes their authority. He protects His word from decay, corruption or human interference. The power of His word is seen in its impact in the lives of those who embrace the call of the gospel. LAMED comes from the term 'to goad' or 'to prick'—God's Word is the source of conviction (in operation with the Holy Ghost), it is untouchable, it stands firm (Hebrews 4:12). The former Saul of Tarsus, on the road to Damascus, so convicted by the pricks of goads of conscience (Acts 9:5), was arrested in his tracks, made submissive to God and served him as a faithful Apostle (Acts 9 onwards).

However, LAMED is the image of the shepherd with the sheep is in view here, leading and prodding the flock to safety (Psalm 23 and John 10). This is how God deals with His people in tenderness but with care, concerned for their souls and the impact of savage wolves, which will harm the lambs.

Down through the centuries of time people have tried to interfere with parts of the Bible, to critique it, to stand in judgment over it, instead of humbly sitting under it. The so called 'Age of Enlightenment', led to individuals treating the Bible as fallible works of men. James Hutton and Charles Lyell, of the 1700s, contributed to the rise of uniformity, where scientific rationalism was used as the standard for assessing knowledge.[24] Such thinking sought to make a complete break away from the scriptures and sought to erode confidence in the revelations therein. None of this changes a single thing. The Word of the LORD is always spiritually relevant to all, across all times, languages, nations and in all places. It is inerrant-this is the character of the Word, that it is pure and infallible-not proved wrong and can objectively be trusted as truth and below[25]. The Bible stands, and will always stand, this because of the words of God are directly inspired 'God breathed', θεόπνευστος, ov theópneustos (2 Timothy 3:16) by the mouth of the LORD and are of the highest purity. Next, the indications of God's faithfulness can be clearly seen in His dealings with man, who perpetually sins against Him, is born with his back towards Him and left to himself, will never seek God. How faithful is God in providing a plan and then way of salvation-prophesied faithfully and fulfilled faithfully. God is trustworthy, we can depend upon Him in all things, especially with our soul, when we pray 'Lord I trust thee with my soul.'

The law (Torah) is said to be a delight to the Psalmist, and if it had not had been, he states in verse 92, he would have perished. An individual who has little or no desire for the Bible is unlikely to be saved or is in a pitiful backslidden condition. It is worth careful examination of whether one is in the faith or not, the hunger of the Bible is a sure marker of being regenerate; without it, it is

24. Garner, *New Creationism*, 78, 79.

25. Geisler & Roach, *Defending Inerrancy: Affirming the Accuracy of Scripture for a New Generation*, 58.

questionable. Without God's Word applied to our lives, we perish. The Prodigal Son, after wasting his inheritance, was brought to a low estate, realised he was perishing without food and came to himself / his senses and thus returned home to the Father (Luke 15:11–32). We must turn to our Heavenly Father who is able to save and then give appetite and food to us from the manna of His Word, oh for a desire for God through the scriptures of truth. Verse 93 is challenging; 'I will never forget thy precepts. . .' God's *piqqud* is to be remembered; His dealings in history are to be remembered as this helps inform us how God deals with His people. Deuteronomy 11:18 instructs: 'Therefore shall ye lay up these my words in your heart and in your soul, and bind them for a sign upon your hand, that they may be as frontlets between your eyes.' The verb, to fix, put in place, tie or gird, are in view when instruction is given as to what to do with the truths of the living God. On account of what God has done for us, making us alive in Him, begetting us, we are not to be forgetful of God's Word: 'I will never forget thy precepts: for with them thou hast quickened me.' The Word of God is the source of reviving the soul. It is sadly true that Christians can be negligent of the reading and heeding of Biblical truths. These things ought not to be so, we should be thankful to God who has rescued us and given us eternal life. He has awakened us up to see our spiritual condition—bankruptcy and ruin before Him and condescended to die and accredit (impute) righteousness to our account on belief of the work He had done for us. George Whitfield, clearly manifest such love for his Saviour, he would read the Holy Scriptures upon his knees; this proved his meat and drink to his soul, for which he daily received fresh light and power from above.[26]

Finally, the writer expresses that he belongs to God: he is a child of His and therefore has different ways, behaviours, standards and an outlook which is entirely alien to those around him. His sins have been pardoned, he had been accepted in the family of God and is a servant of the Lord:

> Fear not, for I have redeemed thee: I have called thee by
> thy name; thou art mine. Thou art my servant; O Israel,

26. Lawson, *Evangelical Zeal.*

thou shalt not be forgotten of me. I have blotted out, as
a thick cloud, thy transgressions, and as a cloud thy sins.
(Isaiah 44:22).

Although the wicked are still prevalent, God is greater, the
Psalmist abides in the Word of God and is shown the evil plans
of his enemies, which will ultimately be brought to nought at the
consummation of the age of grace / gospel opportunity (v.95). In
verse 96, all things are assessed by their transience and limited impact. They are contrasted to God and His ways. Moreover, God's
commandments are 'boundless' (NIV), meaning immense, un-
limited, incalculable or inexhaustible. They may also be described
as,'exceedingly broad' (AV; v. 96), applying to every area of our life,
not just concerned with deeds but the thought life, where lust can
be conceived. Moreover, sins such as hatred, envy, sexual desire,
jealousy, covetousness and so forth are covered by the commands.
The extensiveness of the Bible is that it deals with all avenues of the
Christian life-no stone is left unturned. Equally, the depth of the
mitsvah is beyond the scope of any human literature, something
new can always come from the Word. The precious spiritual gems
of truth are to be sought in earnest prayer.

צז מָה–אָהַבְתִּי תוֹרָתֶךָ: כָּל–הַיּוֹם, הִיא שִׂיחָתִי.	97 MEM. O how love I Thy law! It is my meditation all the day.

MEM, referring to 'what I have'—the Torah is loved and is his
meditation 'all the day'. He loves the Word because of the source
of it and because of the substance of it. By reading the Word, he
then during the day can reflect and think upon its meaning and
when things occur, he has tools to help him. It is a good habit to
begin each day with a clearly defined devotional time, uninter-
rupted period where you can be alone with God. The Lord Jesus
took time to go away from the crowds, and sometimes rising before daybreak, sought His Father. How much more do sinners need
to emulate the Saviour in these things. The blessedness of learning
the scriptures and personally seeking the Spirit to apply them to
you is vital if effective communion between you and God is to be

experienced. The Psalmist could say that on account of his familiarity in the Torah, he was 'wiser than mine enemies' (v.98). His entire paradigm changes when you are converted—he understood more about God through the revealed truths within the scriptures than the heathen around about.[27] This knowledge was essential as he needed to pre-empt attacks and be aware of how to handle their plots and schemes against him. Practical Christianity, which seeks holiness, begins with an experiential knowledge with the Bible—being grounded in the truth.

As a result of seeking to obey God's *eduth*, the author writes that greater enlightenment is shown and understanding more than teachers and the ancients is given by seeking and heeding the *piqqud* (precepts). Moreover, God will not withhold knowledge from the student of His Word and those who diligently seek Him, He will give them understanding. We need to come in a child-like way, with a teachable spirit to the Bible, asking for awareness of God's will for our lives. Against this plea, the prevention of the Psalmist's feet from going anywhere they should not is noted. He explains how his love for the Word (*dabar*), dictates that he will not go to places of iniquity (v.101). Iniquitous places and behaviours are to be rejected; one's feet are to be refrained from following the unconverted populous. As a young believer I remember some people said: ask yourself a question, where you go and what you do, can you in good faith take Jesus there? If the place or event is questionable, should you be there? The psalmist was clear, that, he would not go to places of evil. He would not embrace sin or God would not receive Him, as God is holy. Penultimately, David says he has not 'departed' or 'turned off, aside or out of one's course'; this is the Hebrew meaning from God's *mishpat* (judgments or verdicts). He trusts in them and allows submission to them to shape his life and behaviour.

In closing this stanza, the Word of God, spoken word (*imrah*), is likened to that which is sweet, desirable, better than honey (v.103). Honey may be delicious to the palate, yet God's word makes his mouth water, as it impacts the life and soul. Thus, the scriptures excite the Psalmist, as unlike honey, which provides physical sugar

27. Carson, *Enduring Authority.*

but is a temporary pleasure, the Word of God is life-giving and provides spiritual sustenance and prosperity to the soul. Carson writes: 'The word of the LORD is more than spiritual nourishment, such as a feeding tube would provide. It is a treat that provides enjoyment as well as nourishment.'[28] The term 'honey' is used here and a further 60 times in the NIV, as a descriptor of something most enjoyably sweet. Further, honey is a metaphor for God's blessings (Exodus 3:8,17) and the gospel invitation to come and freely receive (Isaiah 55:1).

The Holy Spirit gives godly appetite for the Bible, which enables us, like babies yearn for milk, to crave the divine truths (1 Peter 2:2–3). Within this illustration, the writer conveys an appetite for the Word of the LORD (rather than sacerdotal and unbiblical ceremony) to gain understanding and combat error, which he finds nauseous. Proverbs 23:23 reminds us, 'Buy the truth and sell it not.' The *piqqud*, details for our lives, is what guides him to ensure that the paths he takes are the providentially good ways and consequently, he hates 'every false way' (v.104). The term 'false' (*sheqer*) denoting falsehood, deception or disappointment. Thus, this governs truth and not our deceptive hearts (Jeremiah 17:9) or the way which appears right to us (Proverbs 3:5–7; 14:12).

נֵר-לְרַגְלִי דְבָרֶךָ; וְאוֹר, לִנְתִיבָתִי.קה	105 NUN. Thy word is a lamp unto my feet, and a light unto my path.

NUN has both a medial arrangement (*kefufah*) and an ending form (*peshuta*), representing God's faithfulness. The scriptures are the medicine for the sick soul, the balm for remedying the soul which lies in sin; God's Word (*dabar*) applies answers to man's greatest needs-pardon for sins and the hope of eternal heaven. The Word is vital, without it human beings stray from God to their own way and follow their own architype. Our nature is corrupt and the residual sin within always seeks to act contrary to God's will. In addition, the world and its values run at variance with God and therefore, our minds can be affected and our feet can take us where it is unhelpful for the child of God to be. Douglas argues:

28. Carson, *NIV Biblical Theology Study Bible*, 1025.

The world is not only a dark place; it is also a dangerous place. Three times in this Psalm remember, the author speaks of his feet. He turns his feet unto the Lord. He avoids all he knows to be wrong.[29]

God's Word provides clear illumination to walk aright without stumbling and guides the feet to avoid walking in darkness. The lamp in Ancient Israel, would have been a common small bowl with a pinched tip used to support the lit wick. The light is referent to illumination / illuminator to guide the path. This image is repeated in Proverbs 6:23: 'For the commandment is a lamp; and the law is light; and reproofs of instruction are the way of life.' The need of the light (Christ, in His book) and the oil (the Holy Spirit) is essential for the Christian pilgrimage. The pathway can sometimes be exceptionally dark, obscured or momentarily, out of sight. In these times, the believer needs the lamp of the Bible to govern each step made lest a wrong step leads to a downfall. Psalm 27:11 echoes this theme of guidance; 'Teach me thy way, O LORD, and lead me in a plain path . . .' The word 'plain' can refer to a straight, right or level way—without obstacles. Crispin notes:

> Through God's enlightening and reviving Word, personal guidance, revival and rejoicing become realities to the person who inclines his heart to perform what God decrees.[30]

David was hunted by Saul 12 times and frequently found himself in perilous situations. However, he could say elsewhere: 'Many are the afflictions of the righteous: but the LORD delivereth him out of them all' (Psalm 34:19). This is testament to the fact his life was characterised with praise and submission to the nuanced terms used for God's Word.

The Psalmist goes on to say how he keeps the ways of God and is conscientious in his obedience; 'I will perform it' and 'I will keep thy righteous judgments' (v.106). Conversion makes all the difference; the believer wants to obey and is grieved when they do not fully do so. He has vowed to obey, here the writer clearly shows

29. Douglas, *Psalm 119*, 153.
30. Crispin, *Bible Panorama*, 262.

love for God and his scriptures. It is a challenge; how much do we love the Bible? It is likely that David's stand for truth causes Satanic opposition; 'For a great door and effectual is opened unto me, and there are many adversaries' (1 Corinthians 16:9). The nefarious, capricious behaviour of the people is manifest in the hour of man and the 'power of darkness' (Luke 22:53). This same attitude resides in children of Satan.

In verse 107, David records how he is severely or vehemently suffering because of his persecutors. This persecution appears to be from instigators of falsehood (as verse 104 denotes how David hates the lies of evil doers). His response is to call upon God and make known his anguish. God refreshes him through His presence as looks to consolation in God through the scriptures of truth.

In verse 108, there is a musical interjection. This teaches us something. In trials, as well as when we feel most able, believers need to praise God. In this verse, he asks God to accept his freely brought praises and teach him the right way. Victory in the Christian life is found in praising God. Psalm 34:1 affirms this: 'I will bless the LORD at all times: his praise shall continually be in my mouth.' David, regardless of the situation (the inscription states how he was in danger before Abimelech), praised God, as He is worthy. His worship was not contingent upon the situation rather he knew that praise was to be 'at all times.' He, therefore, blesses His God. Equally, Psalm 103:1 uses the verb 'to kneel' ('bless') as it summons the soul to praise and prepare for worship and activity. 'Bless the LORD, O my soul: and all that is within me bless his holy name.' All David's faculties are involved—as he contemplates the enormity of God—he summons his soul to praise God.

Finally, knowing the scriptures and doing what they ask are two different things. The Psalmist did not simply want to read and do nothing with what he had read. Verse 109 states: '. . . yet I do not forget thy law'. This is a key to spiritual success and growth in godliness (see James 1:22). In verse 110, he affirms: '. . . I have not erred from thy precepts.' David did not stray from the right path—he was found praising and obeying God. Believers need to be unerring people in faith and living out vital Christianity. Some enjoy talking much in the Christian life but fail to act well in accordance to the truth in Christ. This is not David. 'I have taken thy testimonies as a heritage forever. . .' (v.111). The word 'heritage' can refer to property which may be acquired, a special individual possession or allotted portion. The author notes how God's Word is his possession and obedience to it is his ultimate goal always. The terms 'forever' (v.111) and 'even until the end' (v.112) show the tenure of the commitment the writer has to living out the Word and its truths consistently and always. They shall be taken as a perpetual heritage and left as a legacy to the next generation. Opposite to this, are people who abide for a while and fall away or are zealous for a season but soon forget their commitment to the Word. This was not David; it should be a challenge to live them out fully and pass these revealed truths on:

> And these words, which I command thee this day, shall
> be in thine heart: And thou shalt teach them diligently
> unto thy children, and shalt talk of them when thou sit-
> test in thine house, and when thou walkest by the way,
> and when thou liest down, and when thou risest up.
> (Deuteronomy 6:6–8).

| קיג סֵעֲפִים שָׂנֵאתִי; וְתוֹרָתְךָ אָהָבְתִּי. | 113 SAMECH. I hate vain thoughts: but Thy law do I love. |

The 15th Hebrew letter, SAMECH, refers to supporting or leaning, being upheld by God. Throughout this stanza, the principle of trusting God is enacted. This is contrasted to the wayward behaviour of all the God haters and those who follow futile pursuits. Verse 113 could be rendered, 'I hate vain thoughts' but I love the Torah. Hate, refers to something which is obnoxious, odious or a detestable. To clarify the second part of verse 113: 'vain' (*seeph*) can be translated as 'half-hearted' or 'divided'. The word which is from the cognate noun 'divide' is used elsewhere when Elijah challenged the people at Carmel: 'how long halt ye between two opinions' (1 Kings 18:21). The divided, disunited, half-hearted or futile thoughts that can occur in life are rebuked and in place of this God's Word is lifted high in his estimation. The importance of having a daily open Bible as this guides the way to what is right. Next, the Psalmist affirms that God alone is the one to whom he goes for hiding—shelter and protection from evil persecutors (verse 114).

The Psalmist makes a militant stand, expressing the desire he has to stand for truth in a dark day come what may: 'Depart from me ye evil doers: for I will keep the commandments of my God' (verse 115). He desires the wicked to leave him, as their influence is unhelpful, ungodly and weary.

Matthew Henry writes:

> The more we love the law of God, the more watchful we shall be, lest vain thoughts draw us from what we love. Would we make progress in keeping God's commands, we must be separate from evil-doers. The believer could not live without the grace of God; but, supported by his hand, his spiritual life shall be maintained. Our holy security is grounded on Divine supports. All departure from God's statutes is error, and will prove fatal. Their cunning is falsehood. There is a day coming which will put the wicked into everlasting fire, the fit place for the dross.[31]

David, in verse 116, petitions God for divine intervention. His hope is found in God Himself and His Word. He requests: 'let me not be ashamed of my hope'. As God upholds, gives instructions and shows great love, how our hearts bubbled over: 'And hope maketh not ashamed; because the love of God is shed abroad in our hearts by the Holy Ghost which is given unto us' (Romans 5:5). Once again, the importance of holiness is conveyed by clear referent to the Word. This is where instruction lies and where God may be learnt about. David makes an appeal to the LORD to appear for him in bringing the promises contained within to fruition.

This section closes by affirming that God will destroy the works of the evil ones who will not submit themselves to God and His Word. They will be 'trodden down' (v.118), trampled beneath the feet of the righteous. A clear example of this is Jezebel, a Phoenician princess, who lived an opulent lifestyle in which she persecuted God's people. However, as an act of judgment, in 2 Kings 9, she is thrown to her death and is trampled underfoot. The ungodly are also

---

31. Henry, *Matthew Henry's Online Bible Commentary.*

put away: 'Thou puttest away all the wicked of the earth . . .' (v.119). The unrepentant will be discarded by God like 'dross' (v.119), literally 'slag' or 'refuse', rubbish or waste material. The referent is that their evil will cease and they will be ultimately destroyed.

Against these solemn reminders the writer re-states his love for God and the truth: he trembles in filial fear. Verse 120 states: 'My flesh trembleth for fear of thee and I am afraid of thy judgments.' Carson suggests the Hebrew description for 'fear' means 'stood on end', like the hair which stands up, his 'includes holy fright at the Lord's grandeur.'[32] To postulate, I suspect that a key problem with modern evangelicalism is the lack of the reverential fear of God. We do not shudder at the fear of breaking God's Word. We are not equals or can do as we wish without consequences-judgment suspended or delayed is not the same as that it will not occur. Psalm 50:22 solemnly declares 'Now consider this, you that forget God, lest I tear you in pieces, and there be none to deliver.' The guilt of the people in the fiftieth psalm was refusal to think about God with reverential fear or merely in a human perspective.

קכא עָשִׂיתִי, מִשְׁפָּט וָצֶדֶק; בַּל-תַּנִּיחֵנִי, לְעֹשְׁקָי.	121 AIN. I have done judgment and justice; leave me not to mine oppressors.

AIN begins with the affirmation of who God is—holy and righteous. He acts with equity in all His ways. David affirms God's work in his life, stating he has sought God's righteous ways. On account of this, he appeals to God that he will not let his oppressors have dominion over his soul. The term 'oppressors' in verse 121 means to take advantage of others, especially those who are less privileged. The writer pleads to God that he would not be left to those who treat him abominably. 'Be surety for thy servant' (v.122) is 'to be involved', the guarantee—to take responsibility for, like a person who pledges to fulfil the debts or obligations of another. An Old Testament story which illustrates this point is, Boaz who entered into a contract of being a kinsman redeemer for Ruth (Ruth 4). In the New Testament, a far greater than Boaz is the Lord Jesus Christ, who paid, in

---

32. Carson, *NIV Biblical Theology Study Bible*, 1026.

Himself, all legal accusations we had accrued to redeem His people (Colossians 2:14).

From verse 124 to the close of this section, 128, the thrust of the psalm intensifies. He first appeals to mercy, the only ground to which we can come to God—these are the terms and conditions of entrance into the kingdom of God. 'Deal with thy servant according unto thy mercy' (v.124); the mercy of God is specifically seen in the person of God and ratified in the perspicuity of His Word. Next, he reminds God and others that he is a child of God. Perhaps he does this to reinforce the need of God's intervention and protection based upon God's covenant of mercy and compassion?[33] Verse 125 notes, 'I am thy servant', in this he recognises the position that he is in and asks that understanding may be granted him by divine revelation. The Psalmist asks for 'understanding' that he may 'know thy testimonies' (v.125). The believer can understand (by the work of the Spirit) the Word as those who have saving faith will accept the authority of scripture but those who do not possess such faith will not believe the God of the Bible and can feel a liberty to break its commands (1 Corinthians 2). It is important to note the study of scripture is not anti-intellectualism or acceptation of demonstratable false claims—Daniel, Ezra, Paul are some examples of scriptural scholars. Equally, Francis Bacon, an imperialist of the scientific revolution (1561–1626), argued for the importance of studying the depth of philosophy to lead one to the knowledge of religion. Other notable scholars include Dun Scotus (Augustinian theologian, 1266–1308) who produced a book on the existence of God. In addition, Thomas Aquinas (1225–1274) was greatly influential arguing for natural reason and faith and William of Ockham (1287–1347) who produced a number of sizable works on logic, religion and science.

A parallel between the Psalmist's desire to know and appreciate God's Word is starkly contrasted to the actions of the wicked. On account of this, a rousing call for revival and God's dramatic intervention is deemed necessary: '*It is* time for *thee*, LORD, to work: *for* they have made void thy law' (v.126). The term 'void' is

---

33. Sproul, *The Reformation Study Bible*, 863.

to have done away with, torn up, desecrated the sacred standard. The word 'they' is likely unbelievers who have not experienced the inward work of the Holy Spirit and submit to scripture. Although the initial context is personal deliverance, hermeneutically, this can be applied to calling upon God to revive us again. The nation is at a low ebb spiritually, there are many who are completely ignorant of the teachings of the Bible and are simply indifferent to spiritual matters, how we need to pray for conviction of sin to come to the consciences of individuals in the power of the Holy Spirit. The hand of God is not incapable of doing this, it is my firm conviction that we need to seek God for a local or national revival, it truly is the only hope for this nation. Historically, The United Kingdom was a country of the book, the Bible, with strong conviction and influence in society.[34] These things have long gone and like a shell on the sea shore where a living creature once was, there we see the state of Christianity, like a vacuous seashell. This cannot be worked up but if we loved God and His ways more than 'fine' (or pure) gold (v.127), we would be better positioned to entreat God for such a move of His Spirit once again. David loved all of God's word before lots of money (in verse 72 or before greatest slabs of refined gold). Such value were the scriptures that they were esteemed better than monetary gains.

Finally in this section, verse 128 reminds believers to value and adhere to the Bible as this keeps us on the path of righteousness and is a safeguard against error. All falsehood, experiences and doctrine which do not align with scripture are repugnant. Some teachings have surface appearance of being right but are erroneous—these are to be rejected, the Psalmist could say: 'I hate every false way' (v.128).

קכט פְּלָאוֹת עֵדְוֹתֶיךָ; עַל-כֵּן, נְצָרָתַם נַפְשִׁי.	129 PE. Thy testimonies are wonderful; therefore, doth my soul keep them.

This section begins with the Word of God viewed as a prized possession; PE refers to a mouth (see verse 131). The Psalmist's

34. Burrows, *Our Priceless Christian Heritage*, 313.

thoughts are moved towards the truths within the scriptures. As he longs for more of God so his soul is inclined, like the bias on a bowl, leaning towards the jack directing the bowl. In a similar manner, David delights in knowing a deeper, more meaningful relationship with God. The word facilitates this, going forth provides instruction and invitation, it lights the way, as in NUN. It further provides knowledge of God to the 'simple' (v.130). This is those who humbly submit to the written and spoken truth, coming in a child-like faith to what is heard are those who find great blessing. By contrast, they who come with a proud, conceited spirit will not receive from God.

The exposition of the scriptures provides illumination and assists by enlightening the soul. The scripture propounds 'The entrance of thy words giveth light; it giveth understanding unto the simple' (v.130). The 'entrance' ('unfolding' or 'opening') of God's truth as a prerequisite to obtaining light. Therefore, entering into the Bible and hearing it faithfully expounded allow an entrance to illuminate the soul (to convict of sin in the darkness and reveal facets of the treasures in different verses). Jesus spoke of entering in the door to eternal life, not standing outside listening. In the same way, we must enter into the scriptures by faith and prayer (that the Holy Spirit would reveal divine truths and transmit them to our understanding). The 'simple' are those who are not naïve but teachable and open minded towards the truths of the Bible.

In verse 131 David notes: 'I opened my mouth, and panted: for I longed for thy commandments' (*mitsvah*). An appetite for the Word of the LORD is met with being fed by the God of the book. God will do so at your ability to comprehend truth, beginning with the basics and working towards the depths of truth-pictorially illustrated by milk then meat (1 Corinthians 3:2; Hebrews 5:12–14). The panting for the Word is a beautiful thing, longing that it may feed him and do him good. The image of the woman in labour pains are images portrayed here, suggesting 'a metaphor for strong desire.'[35] A similar image can be seen in the deer who pants for the water brook for refreshment and to take off the scent so that it cannot be hunted down as prey (Psalm 42). He longs, with great desire for the

---

35. Carson, *NIV Biblical Theology Study Bible*, 1027.

Word of God, that it may lighten his soul and assist his pilgrimage. Spurgeon writes: 'An enlarged desire is one of the first fruits of an understanding given to us from the Lord.'[36] May we cry to be fed with the truth.

Following on from this verse, the writer now seeks God again in mercy (v.132), asking for God to look upon him as previously. This indicates in the life of a Christian, there are times of intense blessing with the sense of the nearness of God and at other times, feelings are not as apparent and we operate much more by faith in the promises of God. He consequently asks God to 'order', direct or establish his steps in the Word (v.133), with the primary root meaning of 'being made firm'. To 'order' (or arrange, direct, firmly establish or keep steadfast) indicates David's desire to live life in the right way—with divine alignment—both spiritually (at the centre of God's will) and morally (in purity). His feet are to be established in a steady way; David asks that he might be kept 'in' or 'by' the words of his God. The establishment, preparation or erection of his feet towards the teachings of God is sought. The verse infers that the steps he takes are planned by the pattern of God in accordance to His determined and settled will. Embedded within the second part of this verse is the plea, 'let not any iniquity have dominion over me'. Iniquity can take dominion, command or control when lusts are given into over a period of time and not sincerely repented of. Therefore, knowing the importance of not allowing lust to hatch its viperous eggs, he asks God for power over the force of iniquity. Spurgeon writes:

> Believers should have no pet sins to which they would not be willing to bow. They pant for perfect deliverance from the dominion of evil, and being conscious that they cannot obtain it themselves, they cry unto God for it.

The final portions of the stanza are a call for deliverance from subjugation of men, that he may heed God's ways. In this he supplicates God to be radiant towards him, in showing favour, 'make thy face to shine upon thy servant. . .' (v.135). The link between this and the Aaronic blessing is apparent (Numbers 6:25–26). The

36. Spurgeon, *Golden Alphabet*, 216.

correlation between obedience to God's statutes (*khoke*) and walking aright within the boundaries of this are clearly in view when seeking God's favour.

Finally, 'rivers of water run down mine eyes, because they keep not thy law' (v.136). David employs graphic imagery of eyes flowing with tears; .he is brought to shed streams / channels פֶלֶג of tears in response to the evil before him. His eyes are washed with genuine tears as he sees the progress of the wicked as they advance towards the eternal hell—the caverns of the lost. The prophet Jeremiah wept sore for God's people who rebelled against the words God gave him by inspiration, he wept 'day and night' (Jeremiah 9:1). Equally, he said of how his soul would privately weep within if in pride the recipients of God's message would not adhere to it. In C.S. Lewis' early life, he become deeply impressed, not with endless debates or not, but by a servant of God with conviction:

> He was moving towards Theism, and we had endless arguments on that and every other topic whenever we were out of the line. But it was not this that mattered. The most important thing was he was a man of conscience.[37]

David, clearly was a man of such conscience-grieved when God's standards (contained within the Torah) were not maintained. Believers ought to be people of conviction, concerned for the glory of God within the dark days we live in.

קלז צַדִּיק אַתָּה יְהוָה; וְיָשָׁר, מִשְׁפָּטֶיךָ.	**137** TZADE. Righteous art Thou, O LORD, and upright are Thy judgments.

The letter for TZADE looks like a fishing hook or trap, from the root '*tzod*', to capture, trap or hunt. It is likely that the Psalmist felt hunted and hounded like an animal (themes expressed in a non-exhaustive list of other Psalms: 7, 27, 31, 34, 52). God's dealings with man, the *mishpat*, are always righteous, fair and just. Verse 137 highlights God's rectitude in person and word. God desires His people recognise that in Him and seek to follow righteousness.

37. Lewis, *Surprised by Joy*, 222.

The life committed to holiness (obedience and humble submission to this) often brings about an uncalled persecution (2 Timothy 3:12). However, the Psalmist, although he may not be able to see the footsteps of divine dealings, can express that he knows God is to be trusted in all He does (*mishpat*). He declares that He is faithful in His nature and acts towards him. The NIV for verse 138 renders: 'The statutes you have laid down are righteous, they are fully trustworthy.' The underlying meaning is that God's teachings and ways manifest equity and great, or exceeding, faithfulness.

When witnessing violations of God's commands, he was moved with zeal for rectifying this. Verse 139 says: 'My zeal hath consumed me, because mine enemies have forgotten thy words' (*dabar*). The term '*quin'ah*' (for '*zeal*') expresses strong passion, often transliterated as jealousy. We may think of the Lord Jesus, who overturned tables in righteous anger. Here the author is 'consumed' by fervency for the kingdom of God's sake on account of the adversaries being negligent of keeping the Word. The Dake Annotated Reference Bible gives examples of individuals who manifest zeal for God's glory:

- Moses (Exodus 2:12; 11;8; 32:19–20)
- Phineas (Numbers 25:7–13)
- Joshua (Numbers 11:27–29; Joshua 7:6; 8:28)
- Gideon (Judges 6:11–32)
- Samuel (1 Samuel 12:23;15:11, 35; 16:1)
- David (2 Samuel 6; 7:2; 8:11–12)
- Jehu (2 Kings 9–10)
- Jesus (John 2:17)
- Peter (Acts 2:14–40; 3:12–26)
- Paul (Acts 9:20; 18:5–6; Romans 9:3).[38]

The term clearly refers to protective, righteous jealousy for the truth of God's standards and His holy name.

---

38. *Dake Annotated Reference Bible*, 1008.

The Word is 'very pure' (v.140), meaning 'tried' or 'refined'. The ESV translation renders this part of the verse—'Your promise is well tried . . .' Moreover, 'tsaraph' means to 'be tested', the Word has been proven as true and trustworthy. No word ('rhema' in the Greek New Testament) of Yahweh will fail, every promise He makes will be fulfilled as it is true (Luke 1:37). God's promises are true and tested—they are unfailingly accurate and can be depended upon. Three pertinent cross-references which accentuate this include:

> 'As for God, his way is perfect; the word of the LORD is tried: he is a buckler to all them that trust in him.' (2 Samuel 22:31).

> 'The words of the LORD are pure words: as silver tried in a furnace of earth, purified seven times' (Psalm 12:6). 'The statutes of the LORD are right, rejoicing the heart: the commandment of the LORD is pure, enlightening the eyes' (Psalm 19:8).

All other works, however great, do not surpass the purity and depth of the Bible—this is why it is the most noble of our meditations. The validity and reliability of the scriptures in the truths conveyed—the doctrines, science and historicity are inerrant. The purity of the Word is likened to silver refined seven times (Psalm 12:6), without alloy, imperfection and impurity. Against the overlay of this notion, the Psalmist has every confidence that the Word can fulfil its purposes—teach, instruct, rebuke, direct, train and be a sure guide in life and death to assist the pilgrim to heaven. Moreover, the Word of God is likened to the double-edged sword (Hebrews 4:12). The sword which cuts in both directions and is exceptionally sharp, penetrating, severing and discerning, opening up the heart to our need to drive us to Christ. All things are open and naked before such the God of the Word. The sword is likened, in the Greek, to being at the windpipe to 'open' (v.13), a term used for being at the neck for operational or beheading purposes. In this, if we fail to submit to the written Word and thus the God of it, we will be exposed for what we are, but if submissive, it will open us up to the sword which heals, making the wounded whole, and drives us to God.

The stanza closes by stating how he felt insignificant (v.141) and was subject to ridicule by those outside of the faith. It is the lament of the writer to say he felt 'small and despised'. Sometimes, the opponents of God's work can seem so big and we, by contrast, so small and unable to help. However, although from Sunday School, many have been taught the story of David and Goliath, David at the time did not know the outcome when faced with a giant (approximately 9 feet tall) from Gath defiling the name of his God. David was small and youthful, whereas Goliath was overpowering and blasphemous to this young man-humanly the giant would win. 1 Samuel 17 records a different outcome, that David comes in the name of JEHOVAH against the Philistine, and with some smooth stones and a sling destroys the champion. God uses His methods to destroy the seeming powerful works of the enemy. It is the solace of the Christian that one day God will put all things right. It is important to be on the right side of judgment. Revelation 6 records how unbelievers will desire to be buried in the mountains and rocks than face God's burning vengeance.

> And the heaven departed as a scroll when it is rolled together; and every mountain and island were moved out of their places. And the kings of the earth, and the great men, and the rich men, and the chief captains, and the mighty men, and every bondman, and every free man, hid themselves in the dens and in the rocks of the mountains; And said to the mountains and rocks, Fall on us, and hide us from the face of him that sitteth on the throne, and from the wrath of the Lamb: For the great day of his wrath is come; and who shall be able to stand. (Revelation 6:14-17).

Finally, God's name is honoured, he affirms God's law as truth. In a day where people seek meaning and truth, the Bible remains consistent and unchanged. People have tried to erase the standards of the LORD from scriptures and re-write, or re-interpret parts they don't wish to submit to. The Psalmist notes 'thy law is truth' (v.142). Truth is not relative, it is consistent like the nature of the immutable, eternal, omnipresent, omniscient God to whom we all must come. Pontius Pilate asked, scornfully, what truth was before heading out to give his fallible judgment on the incarnate Son of God (John 18:38).[39] Each of us must come and recognise the truth as it is in Christ before it is too late and we turn away like Pilate did and are eternally damned.

The last two verses (143 and 144) of this psalm show how perplexed the writer was—the terms 'trouble' and 'anguish' are used to describe something of the inner pain he felt. Verse 143 expresses 'Trouble and anguish have taken hold on me: yet thy commandments are my delights' (*mitsvah*). The word for 'trouble' (*'tsar'*) can be deemed as 'narrow' or 'tight'. This highlights the squeezing of the child of God by means of trials. Peter writes of the 'fiery trial the believers were facing was evidence of truth faith and had a sanctifying effect (1 Peter 4:12). Nonetheless, the believer can sometimes feel overwhelmed; the Hebrew for 'overtaken' or 'taken hold' in verse 143 indicates these problems 'found' him. Even though he underwent such experiences, he remained true to the One who was always faithful to him—the LORD. Such a testimony confounds the world as they cannot understand why a person can be joyful when they have their back against the wall. Paul writing to the Corinthians notes: 'As sorrowful, yet always rejoicing; as poor, yet making many rich; as having nothing, and yet possessing all things (2 Corinthians 6:10). The section closes with, 'Give me understanding, and I shall live' (v.144), this is a prayer for the gift of spiritual insight and to be kept from self and sin—the great enemies of the soul. Spiritual understanding of God's will and purpose will enable the soul to live and walk in obedience to His revealed will.

קמה קָרָאתִי בְכָל-לֵב, עֲנֵנִי יְהוָה; חֻקֶּיךָ אֶצֹּרָה.	145 KOPH. I cried with my whole heart; hear me, O LORD: I will keep thy statues.

The 19th letter of the Hebrew alphabet is 'KOPH', the word for holiness (*kedushah*) is closely linked to this letter. A key aspect of holy living is, as verses 145 and 146 stress, the whole-hearted devotion to God that He might hear and answer prayer. 'I called' or 'I cried,' in Hebrew, is an autobiographical reference to cost being

39. Andrews, *Your Word is Truth: Being sanctified in the truth*, 4.

met with God, a personal, intimate soul experience. Moreover, he vows to hear and keep God's Word and observe the 'statutes' (*choq*), testimonies and principles taught. The whole heart is to be engaged in the worship of JEHOVAH. David says that his heart is not distracted by the cares of this life that devotions are consumed or are minimal lip-service offerings. The entire heart ('whole' translated '*kol*' means 'to avoid stiffness'). Moreover, the stiff neck and cold heart are to be evaded—a warm heart needs to be exercised in the worship of God.

The Psalmist rises early (before sunrise, dawn or dusk) to seek the LORD and wait for His answer in the scriptures: 'I prevented the dawning of the morning, and cried: I hoped in thy Word' (v.147). The Hebrew word for 'dawning' of the morning can be translated 'breath', like the breeze which blows as the sun rises and sets. The Lord Jesus is recorded to have risen early and pray in secluded places: 'And in the morning, rising up a great while before day, he went out, and departed into a solitary place, and there prayed' (Mark 1:35). The challenge to believers in the world of business and technology, do we rise early to seek God in the secret place? David did, he sought to keep the practice of private prayer and before the watch cry, he prayed and cried to God.

The Jews divided time into military watches rather than hours, the Psalmist writes of staying up late, awaking at different watches of the night. It is apparent that he is meditating upon the Word, letting it fill his life, heart and soul and change him; 'Mine eyes prevent the *night* watches, that I might meditate in thy word' (v.148). The writer stays awake, anticipating meeting with His God. Specifically, he reflects upon the promises of God in His Book through periods in the night, perhaps arising and on his bed? His manna was the meditations he made upon the scriptures. Jesus, as the manna of heaven, is the blessing to every seeking soul and the writer should encourage us to spend our time and energy reflecting upon the bread of life. The Lord spoke of labouring for the meat which does not perish—the eternal, heavenly food and work of God (John 6:27). The blessing of 'praying continually', as the injunction in 1 Thessalonians 5:16 is given, allows our thoughts to be about Him and not consumed with lusts, worries or worldly matters. This can be testing for the child of

God who is experiencing 'mischief' (v.150) or 'planned wickedness' (*zimmah*) at the hands of his enemies. However, the promise of God is that He will draw near to those in trials. Today, although this time of COVID may prove to be challenging, God's word provides a great source of inspiration and solace. The word is true (v.151). Deliverance may appear afar off but God's will is being performed. He is accomplishing His purpose and the refining of His people. Penny explains God's ways and timings in prayer are not ours: 'His timescale is quite different to our and what we may wish to be done may be better delayed (1 Peter 3:8–9).'[40]

קנג רְאֵה־עָנְיִי וְחַלְּצֵנִי: כִּי–תוֹרָתְךָ, לֹא שָׁכָחְתִּי.	153 RESH. Consider mine affliction and deliver me: for I do not forget thy law.

'*Resh*' means 'the head' or 'the beginning'. John 1 deals with the word 'incarnate' Christ as God who is above all things and the creator of all things. Likewise, Christ as the head of the invisible Church (of which saving faith is the legal instrument to which one is justified by receipt of the atonement applied to the soul) is the great theme of many of the prison epistles, such as Colossians chapter 1 (the pre-eminence and Lordship of Christ).

In these Paul writes, sometimes in chains, bound for the gospel's sake, yet exalting the name of His God. In this psalm, despite earnest prayer, David reports how he is still troubled by the enemies, blacken his character by lies, these people have put salvation away from themselves (v.155). He appeals to God and notes how he will not give up, free wheel even when on a hard path. David's enemies' attitude wounds him deeply and cries for a fresh touch from God ('quicken' is used three times in this stanza, verses 154, 156 and 159). Moreover, in David's lifetime, he faced multiple difficulties including being hunted by Saul nearly to the point of exhaustion. David, however, does not spend a significant proportion of his time lamenting. His lips are often found with praise upon them. He writes in another acrostic psalm: 'I will bless the LORD at all times: his praise shall continually be in my mouth. My soul

---

40. Penny, *A Study Guide to Psalm 119*, 90.

shall make her boast in the LORD: the humble shall hear' (Psalm 34:1–2). He prays 'deliver me' (v.154), in so doing he uses '*gaal*', meaning 'redeem' (different to the term 'deliver' used in verses 134,153 and 170). Thus, this is pointing forward to Christ's efficacious, redemptive work upon the cross of Calvary. He does not appeal to self-defence but asks God to defend, argue or champion his cause. Sproul writes: 'The Psalmist asks the Lord to intercede for him before his enemies.'[41] This is what the Christian must do, trust wholly in the blood of Christ for salvation and deliverance.

As an interjection, in verse 156 (similar to verse 149) David pleads the mercies of God and reflects upon the immensity of God's kindness. He notes how he does not deviate from the commands as so doing would lead to spiritual decline and waywardness (v.157). In this the writer expresses a clear vision that soon God will appear for Him and what is really important? Keeping steadfastly the scriptures of truth. An eternal perspective can sometimes help in trials, as it reminds us that they are temporary, for a season and ultimately, if they do not repent, they will be judged. 1 Thessalonians 1:7–8 states:

> And to you who are troubled rest with us, when the Lord Jesus shall be revealed from heaven with his mighty angels, In flaming fire taking vengeance on them that know not God, and that obey not the gospel of our Lord Jesus Christ.

Approximately ten years ago, I worked for a line manager who was an agnostic. It felt like she took every opportunity she could be express her disdain for the gospel. This caused me much distress and created an inconducive working atmosphere. After four years, I became unwell, resigned and sought employment elsewhere. I remained in contact with some of the staff and was informed that, on advice of her doctor, she was to relinquish her responsibilities. I felt saddened by this but was reminded that God may have removed her from her position; He 'changeth the times and the seasons: he removeth kings, and setteth up kings: he giveth wisdom unto the wise, and knowledge to them that know understanding' (Daniel 2:21).

41. Sproul, *The Reformation Study Bible*, 865.

In verse 155 'Salvation' is said to be 'far from the wicked' on account that they do not desire to seek God or His ways. The inclination of the heart is against God and His ways. Man, in his natural state, will not come to God, the Holy Spirit must operate within a heart to quicken the individual to their need of Him and His pardon. Left to himself, man will self-destruct, piling up sins upon themselves and ultimately bringing about the wrath of God. However, God in His great mercy, through the work of the Spirit, can make one aware of their need and drive them to be interested in the gospel and care for their eternal state. This leads to conversion being awakened and drawn to repentance and faith in Christ, as Ephesians 2 records. It is good to pray that God would change the hearts of those who persecute us, as this is what our Lord taught (Matthew 5:44). The Blackaby Study Bible commenting upon verse 156, 'revive me according to thy word' notes: 'Unless revival comes by God's Word it is not legitimate.'[42] This reviving is personal and has applicability for local or national revival but both must be according to the Word of God else lasting change will not occur.

Verse 157 notes 'many' persecutors and enemies afflict the writer. Here, the implication is the magnitude of those who oppose the Psalmist is highlighted. 'Many' is also used in the Greek New Testament in one of the most solemn portions of scripture, warning of the numerous self-deceived who will be ultimately driven from the Lord's presence at the great judgment day (Matthew 7:21–23). Persecutions and situations of adverse extremity do not prevent his loving obedience to God's Word. Hardships have not averted his loyalty to His Lord; '. . . I will not decline from thy testimonies' (v.157). He will 'keep' (v.136) and has 'kept' (v.158) obeying. Moreover, he finds a refuge, a sheltered provision in His God (see Psalm 91). We also read in the well-known thoughts of Romans 8:35–39, providing solace for the afflicted, that nothing can separate the child of God from God's lovingkindness. Verse 158 states, 'I beheld the transgressors, and was grieved; because they kept not thy word' (*imrah*). 'Transgressors'— '*bagad*'—the faithless or disloyal. It is a distinguishing mark of evil, the disobedience to the revealed will of God in the scriptures of

---

42. *Blackaby Study Bible*, 723.

truth. Jesus spoke of those who hate the truth, whose deeds are evil, living in darkness (John 3:19–20). David's heart was broken and his spirit grieved by the faithlessness of those around him, especially in relation to heeding the Word. When people around us neglect God and His Word, our hearts should break and we should appeal to God in sorrow to do a great work. David could say he loved God's *piqqud*, he asks to be made alive in his communion with Him, taking him into a deeper relationship with Him.

Finally, he affirms again the veracity of *dabar* and the rightness of the *mishpat*. The entire volume of scripture is true; the ESV translates this part of verse 160 as: 'The sum of your word is truth.' Therefore, the totality of scripture is true, accurate and reliable. God's truth is timeless and is established from the 'beginning' ('*rosh*', verse 160). Since the beginning, its words continue to be true, as God is a God of truth, who loves truth (Hebrews 6:18). God's word will abide even when everything else is destroyed (Isaiah 40:8; 1 Peter 1:25). The scriptures bless all those, who in faith, believe them and seek to obey what they read (1 John 2:17).

קסא שָׂרִים, רְדָפוּנִי חִנָּם; וּמִדְּבָרֶיךָ (וּמִדְּבָרְךָ), פָּחַד לִבִּי.	161 SCHIN. Princes have persecuted me without a cause; but my heart standeth in awe of Thy word.

'*Schin*', in the Septuagint, refers to the name of God ('Shaddai'). This was often scribed upon the Jewish Mezuzah to remind them of God's presence as they came in and out of their homes (Deuteronomy 6:9; Psalm 121:8). The Psalmist needed such re-assurance of God's presence as 'Princes', in verse 161, those in leadership, were maltreating him. Opposition from those in authority can cause pain, consume much time and have financial implications. Governors and rulers are set in positions of authority by the permission of God (John 19:11). Nevertheless, not all of them are the LORD's. Consequently, some do not give the Psalmist a fair trial. Recently, the Christian Institute has reported on more individuals and businesses being targeted for being intolerant of their ideologies and schemas.[43] Intellectual persecution continues, some having to leave university

43. See *"Reality Check: The Subjective Nature of Hate Crime."*

training courses, jobs or trades on account of their stand for Biblical morality. The trade guilds operating in Revelation (chapters 2–3) records the verdict of Christ upon different churches. Some, like Ephesus, had to fight against pagan idolatry. This meant that if believers did not support a deity associated with their work, they would lose respectability and trade; it is clear that some believers were greatly suffering on account of this. MacAvoy remarks how it is 'heartening' that the Psalms capture, with honesty David's emotions, both positive and negative.[44] This is especially pertinent as he expresses how opposition has affected him perpetually. Swimming against the tide of opposition can be challenging, the writer rejoices in the Word and likens it to one who finds treasure (v.162). The notion of treasure indicates booty or plunder acquired when victorious. Thus, the regard for the LORD's Word is evidenced as he is awed by what it says, it also provides him peace and hope in adversity. The author explains how he has sought to act obediently to what he has read and asks God to bless him. David's heart `standeth' (v.161) in a state of reverence towards God as he waits for God's vindication, using the scriptures to garrison his faith. The challenge of reading with a clear view to obeying what is read is important in growth and maturity.[45]

The juxtaposing concepts of hating lying are placed alongside telling the truth—which for David is found in the scriptures alone (v.163). God is light and all lies create darkness—the opposite of His nature. Lying can be a prevalent feature of life today. Employers can sometimes ask employees to fabricate details, sign things or write or agree with untruths. The Psalmist hates lies as it displeases the LORD. The law of God was a garrison against falsehood and his meditation all the time. As part of reading and reflecting upon the Word of life, the author stated that he praised God seven times a day (v.164). He thoroughly lived to praise God perfectly, at regular intervals, as seven is the number of God's perfection. Practically outworked, if the number is taken literally, devotions may occur as the first waking thought (1), at breakfast (2), during morning coffee break (3), at lunch time (4), during afternoon tea break (5), at

44. MacAvoy, Psalm 119, 14.
45. Manton, Psalm 119.

evening meal (6) and the last closing thought of the day, at bedtime in the evening (7). Moreover, the notion of morning and evening devotions are supported by other scriptural references such as the morning Psalm, 3 and the evening Psalm 4 (see verse 5 of Psalm 3 and verse 8 of Psalm 4). Another way of understanding this, is that it can be taken as a non-literal, proverbial idiom for continually. That his devotions should be scattered throughout the day as acts of love to His Lord. However, it is understood, the same principles of a love relationship apply.

Finally, verse 165 pronounces: 'Great peace have they which love thy law: and nothing shall offend them.' Abundant peace (*shalom*) is divinely granted when David communes with God and there is, as the Hebrew may be translated, 'no stumbling [block]' or relational tensions. The peace noted here is multi-layered, the peace from enemies around about, freedom for a peaceable life. Solomon, David's son, has a peaceful reign and the people lived in safety (free from attacks of the enemy), he also built a dwelling for the LORD: 'During the lifetime of Solomon, all of Judah and Israel lived in peace and safety' (1 Kings 4:25). Had not Solomon known this time of rest, he may have not had the time to undertake such a task. The importance of peace was to fulfil God's plans for him and the nation of Israel.

The second type of peace is the peace of God which is precious as it is a direct consequence for the believer of being right with him, justified by Christ's blood (Romans 5:1). The inner man has a peace that the world cannot give or understand; 'the peace of that passes understanding' (Philippians 4:7). This was especially needful to him as his foes were troubling him. Having peace despite (not because of) circumstances is a remarkable blessing; 'Not that I speak in respect of want: for I have learned, in whatsoever state I am, therewith to be content' (Philippians 4:11).

Calvin summarises:

> Great peace have they who love thy law. If we take the word peace for a prosperous or happy condition of life—a sense in which the Hebrews often employ it—the word rendered stumbling—block, to correspond with it, will be used for adversity; as if it had been said, that those

who love God's law shall continually prosper and retain their position, although the whole world should fall into ruins. But a different interpretation will be equally appropriate, namely, that they have great peace, because, being persuaded that both their persons and their life are acceptable to God, they calmly repose themselves on a good conscience. This tranquil state of conscience, this serenity of mind, is justly reckoned the chief point of a happy life, that is to say it is so, when it proceeds from God's being reconciled to us, and from his fatherly favour shining in our hearts.[46]

קסט תִּקְרַב רִנָּתִי לְפָנֶיךָ יְהוָה; כִּדְבָרְךָ הֲבִינֵנִי.	169 TAU. Let my cry come near before Thee, O LORD; give me understanding according to Thy word.

The final section of this alphabetical psalm concludes with '*TAU*', the last letter in the Hebrew alphabet. '*TAU*' means a 'mark' or 'sign'. A feature of a man of God is that he is marked individual, one who cries against the abominations around him (Ezekiel 9:4–6). The author is resilient and shows a fortitude based upon his God. It can be said that he cries in utter dependence throughout this psalm and in verses 169 and 173. Holiness has much to do with being fully committed to the LORD and His cause, honouring Him in continually seeking Him. Spurgeon notes how David is presented as one who is trembling with fear that his cry may be unnoticed like a child or injured animal. Moreover, he wants God's ear and a grasp of understanding, for which he requests to be directed 'according to Thy word' *dabar* (v.169). The ideas, sentiments and philosophies of men are fallible but true understanding begins with fearing God and asking Him for clarity through His Word. There are 25 Hebrew words for the English word 'deliver'. In verse 170 David appeals to Yahweh for deliverance using the word '*natsal*' meaning to 'rescue', 'recover' or 'pluck out of the enemies' hands.' This term is disparate to '*padah*' (meaning to 'free' or 'redeem') used in verse 134 and

---

46. Calvin, *John Calvin's Commentaries*.

different to verse 153 for which God's gentle rescuing hand is to be sought in deliverance using the term '*chalats*'.

Finally, in verse 171 the Psalmist explains how his lips supplicate God, making petitions for God's favour. David sought to be a good communicant, using his 'lips' (v.171) to praise the master and not use them in any dishonourable way or give mixed messages (James 3:11).

As he praises God, which is described in Hebrews 13:5 as a sacrifice of the fruit of the lips (bubbling with praise), we then see him moved to respond in song (v.172). He has a depth of theology, as his song is not the jingles of men but grounded in God's Word (*mitsvah*). Sadly, the profoundity of doctrine is missing at many shallow modern, so called, 'worship' services. In such instances, will-worship is employed. This can lead to ascertainment style services, focusing upon what pleases those who gather. By contrast, the glory of heaven is adoration of the Lord Himself. The thrice praise of God was the cry of heaven around the throne room of God, 'Holy, Holy, Holy' (Revelation 4:8). Equally, the angels veiled themselves 'And one cried unto another, and said, Holy, holy, holy, is the LORD of hosts: the whole earth is full of his glory' (Isaiah 6:3).

Against the background of prayer and praise, the psalmist uses the weapons assigned to win the conquest. The iterative nature of David perplexed by his enemies is repeated throughout the passage. One explanation, given by Millslagle, is that Hebrew does not have the option of highlighting or capitalising pertinent points, thus repeated them for emphasis.[47] As a seasoned believer, a veteran in the spiritual battles, David prays for divine enabling, 'Let thy hand help me; for I have chosen thy precepts' (v.173). In this verse, God's hand is alluded to as a metaphor for God's strength and ability to protect and rescue.

Honouring the LORD, he notes how he has sought to live in the way of obedience and appeals not to self-righteousness but to God, the 'LORD our righteousness'. If one engages in secret sin, how can they honestly appeal to God that they have 'chosen thy precepts' (v.173) without hypocrisy or guile / deceit in their mouth?

47. Millslagle, *Our Most Valuable Treasure*, 111.

This is of course not so for the writer, who asks God for mercy as he earnestly wants to do the right thing. When I listened to a gospel sermon recently in Brighton, the minister stated that, 'When saved, God gives you a new 'wanter', you want the things he wants and hate the former things you once did.' The Psalmist clearly has a 'wanter' aligned with God's.

In verse 174, the depth of David's desire to know his God is clearly manifest: 'I have longed for thy salvation, O LORD . . .' He uses the word 'longed', indicating steadfast desire to pray and be in God's presence. The term may also include yearning for saving help to praise His God aright. Real blessedness is found in God alone who is the author of salvation. On account of being saved, David delights in God and seeks to offer his praise.

In verse 175 we read: 'Let my soul live, and it shall praise thee; and let thy judgments help me.' Psalm 51:15 offers a cross-referent point 'Oh Lord open up my lips and my mouth shall show forth thy praise.' God's judgments or rules, *mishpat* are there to guide in living and praising the LORD. David asks God that his soul may live that he may praise God, the Hebrew verb can suggest that his heart, and consequently, his tongue become like a bubbling spring praising or answering the LORD. Equally, a psalm by the sons of Korah, Maskil (Psalm 45:1) states: 'My heart is inditing a good matter: I speak of the things which I have made touching the king: my tongue *is* the pen of a ready writer.' The heart is said to be stirred, moved or overflow שִׁיר יְדִידֹת: רָחַשׁ לִבִּי | דָּבָר with a pleasant theme of God. David's request is that God make his soul to prosper. Moreover, this highlights a two fold desire—freedom from his enemies (a sense of felt liberty). Second, a quickening of God's Holy Spirit and a liberty in sensitivity to what God would desire to do through him. David wanted to lay his life on the altar and be a vessel God would use.

At the close of the psalm in verse 176, David infers the importance of reflection: 'I have gone astray' (I vacillate or reel). Chapman states: 'The psalmist brings us back to the sombre reality as he closes this beautiful Psalm—our tendencies are no better than lost sheep.'[48] The word translated 'lost' could equally be described

---

48. Chapman, *Thy Word*, 139.

as 'perishing'. Therefore, he asks God to seek him out and to keep him eternally secure (1 Peter 1:5). In the Christian life, periods of spiritual aridness can occur. Times of dryness and sorrow can cause a believer much anguish.[49] Living near the cross of Jesus Christ is an important remedy when one feels their inclination to roam from the Good Shepherd.

The last part of the final verse of this psalm says: 'for I do not forget thy commandments'. This is a clear expression that the writer will endeavour not to overlook the commands (by sins of omission or commission); on eight occasions the author notes how he will not 'forget' the Word of this great Book. However, whilst residual sin abides, humans tend to stray. Spurgeon offers a beautiful golden thought to conclude: 'Before God, we might be clear of any open fault, and yet at the same time mourn over a thousand heart wanderings that need his restoring hand.'[50]

49. Okpombor, *Overcoming Spiritual Dryness: The Complete Compendium*, 15.

50. Spurgeon, *Golden Alphabet*, 257.

CHAPTER 3

A Summary

IT HAS BEEN THE intention of this book to help you use each stanza to deepen your devotional time, to prayerfully consider each section over 22 days, revisiting it and treasuring the psalm.

This work notes some of the pervasive themes, which have been highlighted for clarity:

First, the book of Psalms itself means praise (as adoration to God's divine excellence). It is well-documented the number of scriptures there are which deal specifically with praise (Psalm 100:4; 102:21; 106:2; 108:1; 109:1; 111:10; 1451:1; 147:1; 148:14; Isaiah 42:12; 43:21; 48:9; 60:6; 61:11; 62:7; 63:7; Jeremiah 13:11; 17:14, *passim*). A central theme of Psalm 119 is *praise* or rejoicing (expressly in verses 7, 14, 171). Such behaviour is not contingent upon external circumstances but overflows from David's devotion to God. In fact, many times David feels hounded by his persecutors, yet he still puts the worship of God as the prime foci of his life.

Second, David's *delight* in the scriptures, better than thousands of pieces of gold or silver (verses 72, 111, 127 and 162). David could have spoken of his (1) family, (2) his work or (3) leisure. However, his chief desire was God's Word. God sometimes, in His love, takes one or more of these things away to wean us away from the temporal. Grief emanates from David's experience of the loss of some these things (2 Samuel 11- 18; 1 Kings 2). His reaction was to cry out to God and trust His Word. Psalm 119 stresses the importance David placed upon the scriptures themselves. They are from God. His testimonies are wonderful (v.129) because they come from a wonderful God. Isaiah 28:29, 'This also cometh forth from the LORD of hosts, which is wonderful in counsel, and excellent in working.'

God's Word is completely dependable; David through the psalm opines his trust in it. Moreover, its words are pure (see verses 7,10, 140, 160, 171 and 175). In a day of cynicism and many publications, some may choose to relegate the Word. However, Psalm 119 reminds Christians of the veracity of the scriptures. These should inform theology, worship, decisions and general behaviour. The populous may have ideas but their thoughts are postulations of men. Rather, the Bible has been directly inspired by God Himself. God's Word is eternally true, trustworthy and dependable (Revelation 22:6). This delight moves the Psalmist to action in the sense of *obedience*, it is not a passive love but active (verse 8 and 11). He appreciates the instructions, directions, ordinances and judgments, seeking to live by them (verse 33). He meditates upon them (verse 15) and has a high regard for them, disliking vanity (verse 113).

Third, having, handling, listening or reading the Word was not sufficient for David. He prized the scriptures and acted in accordance to their instructions. To this end, David uses what is taught and seeks *guidance* from God—to know His will and act in accordance to it. A repeated refrain is 'teach me' (such as verses 12, 26, 33, 64, 68, 108, 124 and 135). This underscores the importance of a teachable spirit, submissively seeking God's will. This principle offers an important point, believers are to seek God's ways and path for them (Psalm 25:4-5). David highly valued God's direct instruction that he would walk according to, and fulfil the plan God had for his life.

The *heart* is mentioned as a repeated theme throughout Psalm 119. Black takes a thematic approach to analysing the use of this term:

- the whole heart (v.2)

- the upright heart (v.7)

- the clean heart (v.11)

- the enlarged heart (v.32)

- the inclined heart (v.36)

- the sound heart (v.80)

- the joyful heart (v.111),

- the pitch of the heart (v.112)

- the prayer of the heart (v.145) and

- the awe of the heart (v.161).[1]

When using this schema to understand the inclusion of the term heart in the psalm, it is clear that these themes appear progressive. To highlight this, as the full heart is engaged in the worship of God, so it will seek purity. Furthermore, this type of receptive heart will understand greater truths. The inclination of the heart, filled with God, is one full of prayer, praise and adoration of God. This is clearly the experience of David in Psalm 119. Moreover, this psalm offers generalisability beyond the singular experience and applicability to every believer, in every age.

Fifth, a further theme is the liberty David expresses in following God's truth. This may appear to be a contradiction in terms. How can adherence to the law create liberty? David feels a sense of freedom in obeying the commandments of His God. Moreover, James 2:12 writes of the 'law of liberty'. Is this a green light to sin? No, rather it releases him from the guilt of sins. This *liberty* helps David appreciate God more and moves him into greater depths of truth.

Finally, David is clearly moved at the awfulness of sin and misery, especially when the enemies of God's Word rail against the truth (verse 136). The thread of *persecution* runs throughout the Psalm reaching a peak when those in authority join in (verse 161). David's attackers hate him for his sine qua non devotions to God and his unswerving determination to promote God's honour above all else. Despite diverse attacks, the Psalmist remains resolute to obey the scriptures and follow his God regardless of what others may say. The opponents of the gospel may rage but their times are evanescent.

1. Black, *Psalm 119—Monitoring the Heart*.

Psalm 119 is known for its perspicacity—it exudes the desideratum of perpetual prayer. Revelation chapters 5 and 8 record the prayers of God's people in pictorial imagery. The deployment of metaphors to help finite beings appreciate the value of our prayers to God. Prayers, aided by the Spirit, ascend to the throne of God and are answered according to His sovereign will. These truths, that God sees and hears, are re-assuring when faced with all types of trials, including living during the current pandemic.

> And when he had taken the book, the four beasts and four and twenty elders fell down before the Lamb, having every one of them harps, and golden vials full of odours, which are the prayers of saints. (Revelation 5:8).

> And the smoke of the incense, which came with the prayers of the saints, ascended up before God out of the angel's hand. (Revelation 8:4).

In conclusion, 'Psalm 119 is an ancient song about the joy of knowing, loving and obeying the written word of God.'[2] It is multifaceted, like the many sides of a diamond, offering beautiful insights as the Word is admired from different angles.[3] This psalm has 198 references to God's Word using various Hebrew shades of meaning. Thus, the literary devices (use of the Hebrew alphabetical layout and oscillation of synonyms) employed within the psalm add to the breadth and depth of the stanzas, each verse teeming with meaning. May God bless you as we end as we began, at verse one: 'Blessed' (supreme felicity) from the Hebrew rendition '*esher*', meaning happy "are those who assiduously and obediently love Him and His Word and 'search out' from the Vulgate, 'his testimonies with all their heart."[4]

'*Grace* be *with all them that love our Lord Jesus Christ in sincerity. Amen*' (Ephesians 6:24).

---

2. LaMattina, *Psalm 119*, 3.

3. Carson, *NIV Biblical Theology Study Bible*, 1021.

4. Neale, *Commentary on the Psalms*, 5.

About the Author

Jonathan Beckett, Ed.D., Ph.D., holds Doctorates from the Universities of the University of Southampton in Education and from Newburgh Seminary in Biblical Theology. Jonathan has studied at the Metropolitan Tabernacle (London) and currently works as a senior teacher and lecturer based in rural Sussex. He preaches at Appleyards Bible Church and takes a methodical, expository approach to Bible teaching.

Jonathan's desire is that people may come to salvation; being 'born again' and praise God for His word (Psalm 56:10). His passion is that Christians may dig, with greater depth, into the precious gems within the Word of God.

Bibliography

Adams, J. *Counsel from Psalm 119*. Simpsonville, SC: Timeless Texts, 1998.

Akin, D. *Exalting Jesus in Psalms 119*. Nashville: Holman Bible Publishers, 2021.

Andrews, E. *Your Word is Truth. Being sanctified in the truth*. Ohio: Christian Publishing House, 2016.

Arnold, B. & Beyer B. *Encountering the Old Testament: A Christian Survey*. Grand Rapids: Baker, 2015.

Ash, C. *Bible Delight, Heartbeat of the Word of God: Psalm 119 for the Bible Teacher and Hearer*. London: Proclamation Trust, 2008.

Barton, J. *A History of the Bible. The Book and Its Faiths*. London: Penguin, 2019.

Blackaby Study Bible: NKJV. Nashville: Nelson, 2006.

Black, J. *Psalm 119—Monitoring the heart*. Precious Seed International. https://www.preciousseed.org/article_detail.cfm?articleID=3642

Beverly-Shea, G. *I'd rather have Jesus*, https://www.godtube.com/popular-hymns/i-d-rather-have-jesus/

Bridges, C. *The Christian Ministry: With an Inquiry into the Causes of Its Inefficiency*. New York: Carter, 1846.

———. *An Exposition of Psalm 119*. New York: Carter, 1827.

Brown, W. *The Oxford Handbook of Psalms*. Oxford: Oxford University Press, 2004.

Bullock, H. *Encountering the Book of Psalms: A Literary and Theological Introduction*. Grand Rapids, MI: Baker, 2004.

Bunyan, J. *The Pilgrim's Progress*. London: Penguin, 1965.

Burrows, R. *Our Priceless Christian Heritage*. London: Wakeman Trust, 2020.

Calvin, J. *John Calvin's Commentaries on The Psalms 119–150*. https://www.bibliaplus.org/en/commentaries/3/john-calvins-bible-commentary/psalms/119/165

Carson, D. A. *The Enduring Authority of the Christian Scriptures*. Grand Rapids, Michigan: Eerdmans, 2016.

———. *NIV Biblical Theology Study Bible*. Grand Rapids: Zondervan, 2018.

Chapman, D. *Thy Word: A Devotional Commentary on Psalm 119*. Safford, Arizona: TRU, 2019.

Cole, E. *The Midnight Experience: A 30-Day Devotional and Study of Psalm 119*. Tennessee: Eden, 2018.

Cox, S. *The Pilgrim Psalms: An Exposition of the Songs of Degrees.* London: Dalby, Isbister, 1874.

Crispin, G. *The Bible Panorama.* Leominster: Day One, 2010.

Dake Annotated Reference Bible, KJV. Lawrenceville, GA: Dake, 2013.

Deakins, M. *Searching Psalm 119: The ABC's of Psalm 119.* Searching The Old Testament. Safford, AZ: TRU, 2018.

De Moss, N.L. *Holiness. The heart God purifies.* Chicago: Moody Publishing.

DeYoung, K. *The Hole in Our Holiness.* Wheaton, IL: Crossway, 2012.

Douglas, J. *Psalm 119. The Complete and Full Orbed Alphabet of Heaven.* Belfast: JC, 2008.

Eerdmans, D. *The Hebrew Book of Psalms.* London: Brill, 1947.

Erben, M. *Biography and Education: A Reader.* London: Falmer, 1998.

Freedman, J., & Geoghegan, J. *Psalm 119: The Exaltation of the Torah. Biblical and Judaic Studies.* Winona Lake, IN: Eisenbrauns, 1999.

Fuhr, R., and A. Kostenberger. *Inductive Bible Study.* Nashville, TN: B&H Academic, 2016.

Garner, P. *The New Creationism.* Darlington: Evangelical, 2009.

Geisler, N. & Roach, W. *Defending Inerrancy. Affirming the Accuracy of Scripture for a New Generation.* Michigan: Baker Publishing, 2012.

Gowens, M. *A Study of God's Hebrew Names.* Shallotte, North Carolina: Sovereign Grace Publications, 2016.

Gruden, W. *Systematic Theology.* Nottingham: InterVarsity, 2000.

Henry, M. *Matthew Henry's Online Bible Commentary.* https://www.biblestudy tools.com/commentaries/matthew-henry-complete/psalms/119.html.

Hirschhorn, R. *Psalm 119: The Supremacy of God's Word.* London: West Bow, 2011.

Human, D. & Vos, C. *Psalms and Liturgy.* London: Continuum, 2004.

Isom, D. *Walk with the Word: Psalm 119 Study Guide: Personal Edition.* London: CreateSpace, 2017.

Keeys, C. *Step by Step: The Big Picture Chapter by Chapter.* Essex: Walk through the Bible Ministries, 2010.

Keller, T. *Prayer: Experiencing Awe and Intimacy with God.* London: Hodder, 2016.

Kidner, D. *Psalms 1–72 Tyndale Old Testament Commentaries.* Nottingham: InterVarsity, 2008.

———. *Psalms 73–150. Tyndale Old Testament Commentaries.* Nottingham: InterVarsity, 2008.

LaMattina, C. *Psalm 119: Your Word Is a Lamp unto My Feet.* London: Independent, 2019.

Lathbury, M. *Break thou the bread of life.* https://hymnary.org/text/break_thou _the_bread_of_life, 1877.

Lawson, S. *The Evangelical Zeal of George Whitefield. The Preeminence of Scripture in George Whitefield's Life.* Orlando: Reformation Trust, 2014.

Leith, N. *Messianic Psalms.* West Columbia: Olive, 2012.

Lewis, C. S. *Letters to Malcolm: Chiefly on Prayer.* New York: Harcourt, 1963.

———. *Surprised by Joy*. London: Harper Collins, 2002.

MacArthur, J. *The MacArthur Study Bible*. Nashville: Word, 1997.

MacAvoy, W. *Psalm 119: A Devotional including Quotes from Charles H. Spurgeon's Devotional Commentary*. London: CreateSpace, 2019.

Manton, T. *Psalm 119: One Hundred and Ninety Sermons by Thomas Manton*. Edinburgh: Banner of Truth, 1842.

Masters, P. *Worship in the Melting Pot*. London: Wakeman Trust, 2002.

McKenzie, S. Kaltner, S. *The Old Testament: Its Background, Growth and Content*. Nashville: Abingdon, 2007.

Millslagle, J. *Our Most Valuable Treasure*. Scotts Valley, CA: CreateSpace, 2017.

Mott, B. *A Commentary on Psalm 119*. Morrisville, NC: Lulu, 2017.

Neale, J. *Commentary on the Psalms*. Vol. 4, *Psalms 119–50*. London: Masters, 2012.

Okpombor, I. *Overcoming Spiritual Dryness: The Complete Compendium*. Tbilisi, Georgia: Kings View Publishing, 2021.

Osborne, G. *The Hermeneutical Spiral: A Comprehensive Introduction to Biblical Interpretation*. IL: InterVarsity, 1991.

Penny, M. *A Study Guide to Psalm 119*. Exeter: The Open Bible Trust, 2001.

Pinnock, C. *Biblical Revelation*. Grand Rapids: Baker, 1973.

Piper, J. *When I Don't Desire God: How to Fight for Joy*. Wheaton: Crossway, 2004.

Poole, M. *Matthew Poole's Commentary, Psalm 119*. https://biblehub.com/commentaries/poole/psalms/119.htm

"Reality Check: The Subjective Nature of Hate Crime." https://www.christian.org.uk/features/the-subjective-nature-of-hate-crime/.

Reformation Heritage Study Bible. Grand Rapids, MI: Reformation Heritage, 2014.

Richardson, S. *The Psalm 119 Prayer/Study Journal (KJV)*. Darlington: Evangelical, 2019.

Rogerson, J., and J. McKay. *The Cambridge Bible Commentary on the New English Bible: Psalms 51–100*. Cambridge: Cambridge University Press, 1977.

Ryle, J. C. *Holiness*. 1879. Reprint, Darlington: Evangelical, 1999.

Smith, Timothy Dudley. "*Tell Out, My Soul*." https://www.music-ministry.org/hymns/tell-out-my-soul/.

Sproul, R. C. *The Holiness of God*. Sanford, FL: Ligonier Ministries, 2017.

———. *The Reformation Study Bible*. Sanford, FL: Ligonier Ministries, 2018.

Spurgeon, C. *The Golden Alphabet: An Exposition of Psalm 119*. Abbotsford: Aneko, 2018.

Tomlin, Chris. "*Indescribable*." https://www.streetdirectory.com/lyricadvisor/song/jewof/indescribable/.

Watts, M. *What Is a Reformed Church?* Grand Rapids, MI: Reformation Heritage, 2011.

Watson, T. "*Christian on the Mount: A Treatise Concerning Meditation*." https://www.gracegems.org/Watson/christian_on_the_mount.htm.

Zorn, W. *The College Press NIV Commentary*. Joplin, MO: College, 2002.

www.ingramcontent.com/pod-product-compliance
Lightning Source LLC
Chambersburg PA
CBHW070827100426
42813CB00003B/515